40 Day Focus

on

Prosperity

Reframing Your Life for

Outrageous Success

by

Dr. Kluane Spake

This book is dedicated to all of you who, like me, are searching for ways to find Biblical Abundant LIFE in more profound and accurate ways.

In times past, God spoke in fragmentary and varied ways to our fathers through the prophets; in this, the final age, He has SPOKEN TO US THROUGH His Son.
(Heb. 1:1-2)

Dr. Kluane Spake, http://kluane.org   http://jubileealliance.com;
http://the-Q.org;

E-mail: spake@mindspring.com

40 Day Focus

When God created the heavens and the earth, our divine destiny was already in his mind! When he created mankind in his image, he deposited a unique divine destiny in each person. His plan is that his people would be blessed as they fulfill their divine destiny. As a result, this will bless the Eternal Creator by fulfilling his dream of paradise.

God has always planned for man to have dominion over his paradise. "Then God said, "Let us make humankind in our image, according to our likeness; and let them have dominion over the fish of the sea..." (Genesis 1:26). God designed mankind for dominion. That means we have been given all the enablement by God to take dominion and accomplish our destiny—as well as his destiny.

Your destiny is the fulfillment of his dominion dream for you. A dominion dream is not complicated, it simply means being an achiever in some sphere (or mountain) of life. In order for you to come into the dominion prosperity of your soul health and wealth (3 John 2), you must discover the principles for an abundantly successful life. God desires for you to have a life of purpose, peace, and prosperity. Your destiny dream requires the coalescing of these three to bring you into the fulfillment of your divine destiny.

One of the great discoveries of mankind is that we have the enablement by God to dream in order to design (or discover) our destiny. Perceiving begins with a divine dream of a divine destiny. But achieving this divine destiny requires change—and most people hate change! They see it as an impediment or frustration to their life, thus making them, in their minds, a victim of change.

In order to achieve our divine destiny, we must become a VICTOR of change. Our divine destiny requires becoming change agents. Achievement always begins in what the mind perceives. If we can perceive it, we can achieve it! Our mind must believe it can achieve change. We have been given dominion over our mind; the ability (indeed the command) to change. "Don't copy the behavior and customs of this world, but let God transform you into a new person by changing the way you think. Then you will know what God wants you to do, and you will know how good and pleasing and perfect his will really is" (Romans 12: 2).

The first steps in this journey begin with the motivation born of desire and the passion to achieve our divine dreams and God's divine destiny. It all starts with changing our negative thoughts about ourselves first. Negative thoughts are impediments to our future. They destroy what God is trying to build and bring out of us. We must eliminate the vocabulary of negative words such as: "I can't, it's impossible, it's too hard, I don't believe, I am afraid, what if I fail?" Instead, we must believe God has success in mind for us, not failure. "Without wavering, let us hold tightly to the hope we say we have, for God can be trusted to keep his promise" (Hebrews 10:23-24).

This requires believing God's view of who he says we are: "For in Christ Jesus you are all sons of God through faith" (Galatians 3:26). "What is faith? It is the confident assurance that what we hope for [that divine destiny dream] is going to happen. It is the evidence of things we cannot yet see... by faith we understand that the entire universe was formed at God's command... So you see, it is impossible to please God without faith" (Hebrews 11:1, 3, 6).

By faith we begin to have positive thoughts. Positive thoughts say: "I can, I will, nothing is impossible, I have hope, my destiny dream will come to pass!" God is all about the possible. When the Apostle Paul was struggling in his weakness, God spoke to him and said, "My gracious favor is all you need. My power works best in your weakness. So now I am glad to boast about my weaknesses, so that the power of Christ may work through me" (2 Corinthians 12:9-10). Positive thoughts are born in faith that comes from trusting God. They are required to achieve his destiny dream for us.

Positivity is essential for change. And we must be willing to change the bad habits that are the true impediments to the future, into good habits that will help us reach the future successfully. "For God is working in you, giving you the desire to obey him and the power to do what pleases him" (Philippians 2:13). "He will take these weak mortal bodies of ours and change them into glorious bodies like his own, using the same mighty power that he will use to conquer everything, everywhere" (Philippians 3:21).

Dr. Kluane Spake has written an excellent book to help us achieve our destiny dream. She explains the how and why in "40 days of Focus on Prosperity." THIS BOOK WILL HELP US ACHIEVE OUR DESTINY DREAMS. This book is beyond a devotional; it reveals the necessary patterns and principles that will bring us the desired prosperity needed to succeed.

Jesus spent 40 days in the wilderness receiving God's plan to build an everlasting kingdom. That was his destiny dream purpose and mission. And now you are a pioneer in fulfilling the destiny dream purpose of God for your life. Go forward End Time Warrior and fulfill your destiny dream!

> *Dr. John P. Kelly,* **Visionary Founder, LEAD (Leadership Education for Advancement and Development), CEO, ICWBF (International Christian Wealth Builders Foundation)** *Presiding Apostle, ICA (International Coalition of Apostles)*

Endorsements for 40 Day Focus on Prosperity

Proverbs 29:19 states *"Where there is no vision (or revelation) the people are unrestrained, but happy is he who keeps the law."*

Of course, we are not under law, but grace, yet in the realm of grace there are governing principles, if you will, laws, which if followed will allow us to achieve goals and dreams. Conversely, if we do not follow the laws or principles of God's Word, we will neither achieve our dreams nor enjoy all that the Lord has for us in His Kingdom.

Dr. Kluane Spake, a long time friend and co-laborer for Christ has written a dynamic book to help us get our focus. *Focus* is a major component of vision, necessary to move beyond the mediocre into full, Godly prosperity. Each lesson provided will move the reader deeper into the wonderful world of prosperity, which, once gained will provide the rich and abiding happiness and joy that God intends for us. Of course, reading alone will not produce the fruit of prosperity, but applying the word received will produce much fruit that will remain. May God bless you as you dive into the revelation provided so wonderfully in *"40 Day Focus on Prosperity."*

Apostle Stan E. DeKoven, Ph.D., MFT, President of Vision International College and Graduate School

*

Dr. Kluane Spake is providing more than just a book with "40 Day Focus on Prosperity"- more than just and interesting read for thoughtful Christians. She has provided a tool for the Body of Christ to move into a new dimension of Kingdom advancement. The great transfer of wealth!

The prophets have foretold it for years while teachers and pastors have been teaching it for a long time. Now, as the time has drawn near for the church to take her rightful place of preeminence on the earth, God has given Dr. Spake a timely, practical and relevant strategy to bring individual believers into a position of influence through wealth building and prosperity.

I highly recommend this book for anyone who desires to walk in greater prosperity for the sake of the Kingdom of God.

Mark Pfeifer, Lead Apostle, Soma Family of Ministries

*

Coming out of Africa, I have seen and experienced first hand the ravaging curse of poverty. Many reasons could be attributed to this blight but I believe the dominant reason is ignorance. Until our perspective about money, wealth and prosperity align with the mind of God, many will wallow in needless poverty.

What an awesome opportunity to go on this forty day journey with Dr. Spake to change your focus and begin to walk the paths of true and enduring prosperity. I must warn you, this book will challenge some old mind-sets and obsolete beliefs. If you hate change, please put this book down, but if you are desperate for a change then read on! You will be blessed.

> *Dr. Frank Ofosu-Appiah, General Overseer All Nations and Living Springs International Churches, President: Institute Of Leadership and Development (LEAD).*
>
> *

I think this is a great book with wonderful revelation for people who are serious about prosperity in the 21st Century. I highly recommend that everyone go through all the 40 days. Wealth creation starts in the mind. Wealth is simply an indicator of how well you are doing in the inner game of life. You need to read this book so that you can become wealthy.

> *Dr. Keith Johnson* The Confidence Coach
>
> *

ExcItement! That's what I felt! What a joy to read this book! What a treat it is! I will read it over and over again. As someone who has spent the last 15 years interceding over the release of Kingdom wealth, I found this book to be an invaluable tool. Finally a balanced approach!

The depth of teaching and the use of scripture for each days prayer focus is astounding. You will finish this book with a level of understanding you did not know you needed. Let us not be a people who perish for lack of knowledge. Read, enjoy, meditate, and participate by drawing from these rich wells of experience and revelation.

> *Apostle Jill Mitchell O'Brien*, Kingdom Connections International, Inc. Houston, Texas
>
> *

Dr. Kluane boldly silences the voice of "gloom and doom" that is paralyzing people worldwide. She skillfully addresses the topic many have considered taboo for Christians: gaining and maintaining intentional and progressive wealth.

In this book, Dr. Kluane systematically lays out God's step-by-step detailed strategy for you to make the much needed paradigm shift to walk in God's plan for your life. Each daily lesson is filled with biblical principles and multiple keys on how to prepare you to walk in the full spectrum of prosperity.

Dr. Kluane is like a detective looking for the missing clue in a case, she leaves no stone unturned. 40 Day Focus on Prosperity not only thoroughly exposes personal hindrances that keep you from success; it equips you to remove these barriers so you are able to live a life of extreme success.

Apostle Tommi Femrite, GateKeepers International, President
Apostolic Intercessors Network, Founding Apostle
*

"Forty Day Focus on Prosperity" is a very timely and invaluable work that will bring results when applied. I have worked with entrepreneurs and people of wealth for many years and this type of book is very much needed to establish the right foundation for building wealth. I would like to recommend her book to those who believe God intends for his people to prosper and be good stewards of the resources he has provided for us. Understanding these principles and precepts are important for acquiring the wealth that He desires for his Body, the Church, and to be able to apply them to real life experiences.

Apostle Buddy Crum, Life Center, Atlanta, GA

*

Now and then we are blessed to come across a book that has the capacity to stir us inwardly. Prosperity: A Forty Day Focus is just such a book. The insights presented by the author were gained from years of diligent study of the Word of God and from vast experience in both pastoral and travelling ministry.

In this challenge to the Body of Christ to arise to God's full provision, Dr. Spake has successfully laid out a strategic discipline for living according to God's agenda in the realm of Biblical Stewardship. I highly recommend this book for personal reading and for small group study.

Eric Vernelson, Sr. Pastor of Living Faith Church, Wilson, N. C.
*

I really enjoyed what you've done here! *40 Day Focus on Prosperity* by Dr. Kluane Spake is a compelling and comprehensive invitation to both discover and experience the abundant life Jesus has made available. As you undertake this stepped focus, I believe you will discover as I did, that there is a layered wisdom that presents itself in cumulative fashion. The power of focusing for a significant season is clear for, "As a man thinks (thinks and keeps on thinking) in his heart, so is he".

I also appreciate the theological balance found here as Dr. Kluane puts things in a "Seek first His Kingdom" perspective. Too much of the gospel of self instead of the Gospel of Christ has been seeded into our thinking and too much of the mind of Madison Avenue has replaced the mind of Christ; here, we have a clear presentation much closer to the truth... that sets you free. I trust that you will enjoy your reading; I pray that you will enjoy God's abundance and "prosper and be in health even as your soul prospers" (3 John 2).

> *Walt Healy,* Founding Pastor, Church of Grace and Peace, Presiding Apostle, FaithNet USA

*

What a "marvelous" book! Dr. Spake's Apostolic Prophetic approach to Biblical prosperity will produce tremendous fruit in this New Day. I highly recommend this book as a study guide to individuals who strive for instructions from God for Kingdom Prosperity!

> *Bishop Marie E. Pines,* Malkut Banah Global Fellowship, Galveston, Texas

*

Prosperity and a 40 Day Focus

Dr. Kluane Spake

"Today will never happen again. Don't waste it with a false start or no start at all. You were not born to fail." Og Mandino

Recently, I've been getting endless e-mail newsletters full of "gloom and doom" about the certainty of economic collapse. Prophets warn people to run to the mountains to prepare for the end of the world. They send dismal messages of hopelessness and discouragement. They speak of quiet desperation and the final pages of our time on earth. The question to ask is, should we join the crowd and panic? i don't think so.

In the midst of this turn in natural circumstances, the Lord continues to speak strongly to me about Kingdom success and prosperity. I think it's time to find out about what the Bible says about genuine prosperity, especially in the tough times.

Many believers are apprehensive about what the Bible really says because the whole concept of money and prosperity has been distorted, wrongly applied, and mis-taught. Many believers are disillusioned by ministries that focus excessively on the topic of prosperity and treat it like a "get rich quick" scheme.

> *"Do yourself a favor and learn all you can; then remember what you learn AND you will PROSPER"*
> *(Prov. 19:8 TEV).*

Yet, HALF of the parables that Jesus told used money and finances as a teaching tool. One third of His teaching concerned money!

In total, there are 2,350 Bible verses about money. This is almost twice as many verses as there are about faith and prayer combined. Jesus spoke about money and possessions more than heaven and hell combined! In FACT, Jesus spoke about money more than about any other single topic, except the Kingdom of God itself.

Why? Because there is a fundamental and distinct connection between a person's spiritual life and their attitudes and actions concerning money and possessions. Often we divorce the two – but Jesus relates the spiritual and the natural together.

This alone should be an indication that we should address this topic more than we do! We need to find the truth about God's intention for our lives regarding prosperity.

Your future is determined by what you decide to do today.

Recently, I began to think about how Christians fast for 40 days for many reasons - -there's an Esther fast, a Daniel fast. Believers fast to know God and to hear from Him. They fast to worship the Lord and for Presence.

Forty

What would happen if you declared a 40 DAY FOCUS on your future? It could be a forty day fast from wrong thinking about prosperity that could totally transform your life. You could take time to find out about yourself and build stronger vision and goals. It could be a time to connect to a Divine idea. A time to re-establish proper mind-sets about prosperity.

> There is great significance of forty days. After the flood, man lifespan was 120 years (3 X 40). Forty represents maturity. Moses lived 120 years (that's 40 years in Egypt, 40 years in the desert, and 40 years leading Israel in their wanderings. Moses was 40 days on the mountain receiving the Law of God. Israel wandered in the wilderness for 40 years. Before that, they were in Egypt for 400 years (40X10). Jesus was born 40 centuries (4000 years) after the Fall, so the world was mature for Him.[1]

How about fasting 40 days from a poverty mind set? (Or 40 weeks if you choose to do a chapter a week.) Maybe you could

---

1.See endnotes for a lot more about 40 days.

concentrate on a 40 DAY FOCUS to learn how to establish true Biblical prosperity into your life? Retirement? College for your kids? Write the answer to these questions here in this book.

Am I totally satisfied and willing to settle for exactly where I am financially right now?

Have I accomplished my destiny and met every goal in my life?

Do I want or need to upgrade my financial future to one of outrageous success?

Am I willing to commit to a 40 day of process of gaining new thought?

Am I willing to think and act with new perspectives that may seem "outside the box?"

When you have a desire to achieve more, it does not necessarily mean that you're unhappy with your current life status. In fact, you've probably experienced many wonderful rewards and achievements... and simply just want to magnify them even more. That's how today can be your new beginning!

Try to do the daily reading and assignments at the same time every day - in a place where you can be still and hear the Lord. Quiet your heart - and hear the Lord speak.

Just do the tasks presented... if you miss a day, just start back up where you left off. It may seem to you that the topics are simple and that you already know them, but please don't read ahead to the next day.

You will want to use a notebook for some of the answers. Each day has what you need to do for that day. Sometimes similar ideas are presented on different days to reinforce overlapping concepts.

You will find when you put these days together that they become a magnificent symphony about a growth experience of getting to know yourself. You will never be the same!

It's about gaining intentional and progressive wealth!

You will notice that there are questions for you to answer and that they are in a lighter gray font. Space is provided for you to write your answers in this book and make it yours! Also, use the margins for your own personal comments and notes.

This book is about reprogramming your mind to know Who the God of Love and Prosperity is IN YOU! This forty day journey is one of self discovery and change. It is about obtaining a correct Kingdom mind-set about dominion and WHY you have Prosperity.

God's Friend & Yours

Dr. Kluane

Focus 40 Days on Prosperity

Section #1, "Establishing New Mind-sets!"

Biblical Truths You Must Know

Your Blessing

The Seed

Day 1 - Focus on Finding the Truth About Prosperity

I called a pastor friend the other day and asked him about this present economic situation and what message he thought his congregation needed to hear about the most! He answered that they need to learn to live like he does – needing nothing.

He explained how he had earned and lived on $4,000. last year! He felt that his church needed to learn to live that way too. Being "humbled" allowed them to better hear the voice of God and care for the lost. "Poverty keeps their priorities right!" he said.

There seem to be three major error messages taught in the Church about Spiritual Prosperity that have caused the believer much conflict.

Old Mentalities

1. Deceitful Riches

It's true that some forms of gaining wealth contribute to corruption and every evil work. The world's ways with money can be grievous. Scripture tells us about the ungodly who increasingly prosper in the world (Ps. 73:12).

- The Bible tells us that "Fools are destroyed by prosperity" (Prov. 1:28-32). Many use their wealth as a fool.

Are riches deceitful? Mammon rules the world and the unfortunately, much of the church. The word 'mammon' refers to wealth and riches -- but the word is rooted in deceitful self-reliance and on the unredeemed soulish accomplishments that leads to a false or man-made reputation (idolatry).

When Jesus told the disciples not to serve God and Mammon (Mat. 6:24), He was not telling them to be poor, but rather, instructing them to not place their trust or allegiance in mammon (self reliance and self accomplishments can be deceitful). God opposes you when you TRUST in money as your SOURCE or objective of life.

"Therefore if you have not been faithful in the use of unrighteous wealth (mammon), who will entrust the true riches to you? (Lk. 16:11). Those NOT faithful in unrighteous wealth (mammon) will not be entrusted by God to use righteous wealth!

An example of deceitful riches is the over-done warped prosperity message. You've seen this in action! These advocates live in lavish personal opulence and have arrogant ideas about themselves. Their extreme extravagance goes beyond the limits of necessity or restraint, stability, and balance.

Most of us know about the unfortunate extremes that many such preachers use to manipulate through greed. We see how they used Scripture about prosperity to become "deceitful riches."

Then, on the other side, most believers think it is spiritual to have a poverty mindset. But... where did all these misunderstandings come from?

2. The Hebrew and Greek World View

This section contains vital information that you need to remember for the whole book!

THE HEBREW WORLDVIEW always looked to the spiritual as being LINKED to the natural. That is how Jesus viewed blessing. Blessings in the spiritual realm *always* meant it affected the natural world.

THE GREEK WORLDVIEW (Hellenistic) of thinking vastly influenced and distorted the whole original Jewish/Hebrew concepts. The Greeks were totally involved with the spiritual realm and believed that spirituality was the only realm that mattered.

The tendency toward religious poverty comes from the Greek worldview where the spiritual is superior to the material/temporal realms in every way.

This Greek worldview strongly influences the Western church today. We still see many mystic type "super-spiritual, heavenly-minded" believers who think we should ONLY be concerned with the spiritual realm (this is a form of Gnosticism).[1]

The idea of poverty being spiritual started after 300 AD (during the Dark Ages) when people did not have access to Scriptures for themselves.

As the influence of Greek thinking increased and dominated the Middle East, so did the idea that poverty and suffering pleased God. (These are usually well meaning and sincere people.)

The early Church Fathers (Origin, Clement, Justin, and Augustine), were all Gnostic (Greek thinkers about the spiritual only). They were concerned with the invisible world, and the realm of thought and truth.[2] To them, the "real world" was intangible - the one of intelligence. The temporal was insignificant.

False piety, asceticism, and mendicant lifestyles have been a way of life in Christian thinking for centuries. Clerics lived in abject poverty, some never leaving their cloistered abbeys or convents. They would torture and whip their bodies and live lives of denial and begging for food. It was all about the evils of wealth and earthly pleasures.

They taught that it is more *holy* to be poor and sick than to be wealthy and well. This Greek mind-set demanded vows celibacy, vows of poverty, and a clergy that was separate from the believers.

1.Gnosticism (gnōsis, knowledge) is a popular belief system during Late Antiquity teaching that the material cosmos was created by an imperfect god.

2. See my book "From Enmity to Equality" for a lot more information on this subject.

They taught (and many still do) about how people who want to be rich fall prey to ordeals and tricks that wait for them. They thought that the desire for riches caused people to only find destruction and ruin.

Biblical Mind-set about Poverty

Looking from the Hebrew Biblical view of Scripture, rather than one influenced by the Greek scholars, we see clearly that POVERTY IS A CURSE. Poverty starts *inside* of a person (belief system) and shows up on the *outside* as a curse (Deut. 28:15, 28:48).

Poverty causes greediness (1 Tim. 6:10), covetousness (Col. 3:5), stinginess, and hoarding.

"All hard work brings a profit, but mere talk leads only to poverty" (Prov. 14:23).

"You have planted much, but have harvested little. You eat, but never have enough. You drink, but never have your fill. You put on clothes, but are not warm. You earn wages, only to put them in a purse with holes in it" (Hag 1:6).

"Why do you transgress the commandments of the Lord so that you cannot prosper?" (2 Chron. 24:20).

A poverty mind-set holds you emotionally captive by an internal vision of failure. Poverty attitudes foster a state of dependence - maybe someone or something else will come along to help me. Luck. Fate. Chance. In general, poverty minded people live from paycheck to paycheck - by the clock, staying in a job they hate, afraid to move on, wanting only job security, and willing to take only a few risks. They are often resentful against those who do well.

Enduring the curse of poverty is a learned behavior. It will determine your future. Do you know that DEBT IS a mindset?

People with poverty mind-sets tend to be more angry, frustrated, cynical, pessimistic, and have smaller goals (mental claustrophobia). Their imaginations are limited, petty, restricted, and confined. Most poor people focus on what they DON'T have and what they DON'T want - instead of what they DO have.

Remember this

You must break that spirit of poverty that hovers around you. Don't allow unproductive and unsuccessful people with old fashioned mind-sets to influence you any longer. As you embrace greater Truth, you are empowered. Poverty is not just about money - it is about your abundant life spiritually, physically, mentally, relationally, and financially.

CAUTION: Be sure and not try to use your faith to obtain things or positions that the Word of God or the Spirit of God has not promised! Presumption can be dangerous ground.

Jesus Reversed the Curse of Poverty

Deuteronomy 28:47-48 says that because Israel did not serve the LORD your God joyfully and gladly in the time of prosperity, they were left in hunger and thirst, in nakedness and dire poverty. Notice that their condition of poverty is described as ...*hunger, thirst, nakedness, and dire poverty*. Now, think about the condition of Jesus on the cross. He was hungry, thirsty, and naked. Jesus became "poor," so that we could freely experience His riches.

Jesus became poor at the cross and took your poverty upon Himself. He reversed the curse (Gal. 3:13, 14, 16, 29).

Spiritual prosperity is a non-negotiable Kingdom principle.

- Since Jesus made such a great sacrifice for YOU, will you apprehend the value of His sacrifice?

- Learning about Godly prosperity in the natural realm is related to the release of the Spirit prosperity in your daily life.

"No pleasure is comparable to the standing upon the vantage-ground of truth." – Francis Bacon

"Poverty is the voice that says, 'God is not able!'" Chuck Pierce

Day 2 - Focus on the Blessing!

Adam was placed in a Garden. It was not just a spiritual wonder - but a natural Paradise. God made the gold and said it was "good." There were rivers and trees. The earth was now *formed* and becoming *filled* so it could *fulfill* His purpose. The Lord developed a precise plan for humanity so that they could bring forth His image and likeness.

Our Original Mandate Is to Prosper and Have Dominion!

> Gen. 1:27-28 *"... And God BLESSED them, saying, "Be fruitful, and multiply, and replenish the earth, and subdue it; and have dominion... over every living thing that moves upon the earth."*

The ability to reproduce, subdue, and have dominion was the BLESSING. It was also a command. God *blessed* the first humans and commanded them to go into a joint venture with Him.

"Bless" means to give favor. According the *Theological Wordbook of the Old Testament*, it means "to endue with power for success, prosperity, fecundity, longevity, etc."

Genesis 1-3 tells us that YOU came from the very breath of God. You carry His DNA. YOU are *already* blessed and created to be a blessing to others. The Holy dignity of God dwells in you and awaits you to personify the blessings He has already given you.

You were created OUT of God with individual destiny!

The Message Bible says, "*God created human beings; he created them godlike, Reflecting God's nature. He created them male and female. God BLESSED them: "PROSPER! REPRODUCE! FILL EARTH! TAKE CHARGE!"* (Gen. 1:27, 28 MSG)

DOMINION was NOT a wish of God, but a personal COMMAND and a PROMISE OF PROVISION.

You were born to take charge and create! God always provides the power and potential for the fulfillment of His commands. It was His original intent that humans prosper.

It was the job of humans to enforce the garden blessing of prosperity. GOD NEVER CHANGED HIS MIND!

The BLESSING of the Lord makes one RICH! Prov. 10:22

THE BLESSING activates your life cycle and the ability to reproduce and have dominion.

- To PROSPER (BE FRUITFUL) was GOD'S very FIRST WORD to any human.

- Disobedience STOPPED the BLESSING.

- The serpent didn't STEAL Adam's BLESSING - Adam gave them up!

- Jesus returned to gain the fullness of the BLESSING back.

- Jesus came to save THAT which was lost! What was lost? The dominion BLESSING.

- God still intends for all humanity (YOU) to walk in this Garden BLESSING.

- The job of humans was to enforce the Garden BLESSING of prosperity in every area.

Your assignment on earth is to adopt God's success philosophy - it's a mind-set that wins! This is your dominion mandate. Notice that it is HAVE dominion (not take). Dominion is there for you to have.

Dominion is about "having" the influence to bring forth the Kingdom.

Don't labor in yesterday's mistakes, create a passion for increase in the NOW. RECEIVE IT NOW...

This is the message of blessing! Wear God's BLESSING daily in your life! The only thing that stops you is YOU and your contradictory thoughts and doubts.

> You *already* inherited the BLESSING! You are *already* empowered to prosper in every area of your life!

The BLESSING of the Lord makes RICH (Prov. 10:22).

THE **POWER** WITHIN THE BLESSING IS THE FORCE THAT BROUGHT FORTH THE IMAGE OF GOD UPON THE EARTH. Nothing can hold back Blessing.

SEE your future now as God partnering with you to achieve the Garden mandate of prospering, reproducing, filling the earth, and taking charge! Gold was part of the blessing...

Write out Genesis. 1:27-28 in your own personalized words.

- This is your greatest hour
- Your inheritance is already yours
- Are you conscious of your treasure?

Salvation

In the original Greek language, full salvation (*sozo*) MEANS WHOLENESS, safety, rescue, deliver, deliverance, health, prosperity, protection, freedom, liberty, peace, righteousness, and victory).

Sozo means to BE MADE WHOLE and prosperous in every area of life - spirit, soul, and body.

Salvation is already here for you - it is not a condition to achieve, but a condition to be aware and apprehend.

To obtain total salvation means you MUST move from the mind-set of survival to that of significance – from the attitude of scarcity to abundance and prosperity.

- You were not created to be average or mediocre.
- God has a big plan for you.

- Salvation means there is something better out there for you. You can make a difference.

- Salvation means you can live a life without debt or discouragement. You have options and freedom.

- Salvation brings you a life of passion and purpose.

The Blessing is for You

"Follow my commands and you will PROSPER in everything you do!" Deut. 29:29

Jesus came to empower the Church with His abundant life (Jn. 10:10). He wants to bless you with empowerment and success. He gives us the same inheritance as Jesus - we are joint heirs.

Do you believe that the God Who lives IN YOU will bless you?

With the riches of any blessing comes the admonition to be spiritually responsible.

You are a member of the FAMILY - You ALREADY have the keys to the "car." The inheritance is yours - it is not just a future promise - but a now reality. Adult heirs inherit now! Abraham was the heir to the world (Rom. 4:13) - think about it!

The church (*ecclesia*) is a military term that means "occupation by revolution, those called out to rule, to govern nations, take the offensive, and live in dominion." The church should liberate, empower, and bring about this CHANGE though the BLESSING.

As the Church, our job is to begin building, restoring and governing. The Kingdom world view is to invade, occupy and influence the world for Christ.

What new thing are you grateful for?

Every day say, "*My life is worth living well*.

Take some positive actions today that will later cause some new results for you.

Day 3 - Focus on The Seed of Prosperity

Ideas, thoughts & visions are seeds. When they are based in God's Bible Love-plan, they are miracle seeds & they will yield or produce after their kind (Gen. 1:11-12). Dr. T. L. Osborn

Prosperity is a Third Day reality!

On the THIRD DAY of Creation, God created the SEED (Gen. 1:11). Now, every living plant that God created has a seed in it and it is supposed to MULTIPLY.

As long as the earth endures, seedtime and harvest will never cease (Gen. 8:22).

Jesus is the incorruptible seed that is planted inside you. Salvation (*sozo*) is the seed of Christ planted IN YOU. *Sozo* includes healing, deliverance, and PROSPERITY. Listen to your heart and discover that the seed of prosperity is yearning and groaning to grow. Salvation always calls us to expand into MORE!

That seed knows HOW to grow. Inside that seed is EVERYTHING that is required to reproduce what it came from. An orange seed grows an orange tree. A God seed grows and God-type person. The Creator's DNA is within you! You are on a Divine mission to unveil the fullness of your salvation!

Matthew tells us about the principle of the seed - and says if you don't understand this, you DON'T UNDERSTAND ANYTHING (Mat. 13:19). That's a serious statement that you can't ignore! The seed of revelation grows and develops. You must exercise your faith and be determined to optimize the growth of your whole salvation.

No matter what is going on right now, the incorruptible seed of prosperous salvation wants to grow. Matthew says that day and night that seed grows and we don't know how (Mk. 4:27). You may not realize it or feel it - but God's Word is true and that seed is growing.

Prosperity begins as a seed. The Bible contains over 2,000 verses on money. That's more than what is said about prayer and faith combined. What the Bible says about money should be an important consideration for every believer. The idea of prosperity should be a seed that you plant in the garden of your heart.

- What is Scriptural wealth? It includes things of value (Ps. 24:1-2) like diamonds, gold, currency, minerals, rubies, silver, live stock, etc. The earth is the LORD'S and everything in it!

- It all depends on what you do with that emerging seed within. It matters how you grow your seed.

- Holding on to the past (and even the present) hinders the growth of that Divine seed. Allow that SEED of salvation to fully mature so that you can fulfill your assignments.

That seed of prosperity has extraordinary ENERGY necessary to reproduce and multiply. If you plant that seed in good ground and water that seed (with the Word), it will grow! Everything in the Kingdom is constantly expanding.

The husbandman patiently waits for the precious fruit of your life to mature and be harvested (Jms. 5:7).

Just like the energy from a growing seed must find a way through the top of the dirt in order to express itself as a flower or fruit, so it is with the delivery of desire. It expresses energy inside of you to bring forth that which was promised. By choosing to follow your dreams, you fulfill your function and purpose on earth.

"It is God that works in us both to will and to do His good pleasure" (Eph. 1:5).

The key is to discern the Divine desire (the dream) that directs you. The more you move toward God's intentions, the stronger desire becomes.

When that which was dead begins to stir to life again, there is resurrection of desire once again in your heart. As you prophesy faith, the once useless, disconnected, bleached, dead bones in your valley begin to reconnect. It is resurrection time! Be alive in God's life for you. Let that Godly desire arise once again. Become the warrior who can release the Kingdom.

Growth of a seed moves intensely toward light and water. Your pursuit must become a predominate force in your life and you must begin to self-manage yourself to get there.

***

"I pray for good fortune in everything you do, and for your good health—that your everyday affairs PROSPER" (3 Jn. 2).

In 3rd John 2, the Greek word for "prosper" is *euodoo* (yoo-od-o) from two root words: 2095, *eu* (yoo) meaning "to succeed, to do well" and 3598, *hodos* (hod-os) meaning "progress in a long journey, to help on the long road, to succeed in traveling a prosperous and long journey."

- The road to prosperity is a journey.
- We don't see every turn on the map of our road - yet!
- It is a successful and prosperous journey.
- The prosperity of this journey refers to material, spiritual, physical, and social prosperity.
- Prosperity is NOT what you wear, eat, or drive. It is not consumerism.

This verse continues, "And be in good health, even as thy soul prospers." Notice that the temporal prosperity is conditional upon your co-existing soul realm prosperity.

Begin today to think and act like you *already* have prosperity - and that money is not a problem. That doesn't mean you get to take a jet trip to Italy this afternoon... But, imagine that you have the ability to change your circumstances. How would you feel? How would you enjoy your life if you could afford to do anything you wanted?

Write about how you *FEEL* about living in prosperity:

Speak to the seed that is already planted in you. Tell it to grow!

"The objective of all life is development. Every living thing has an inalienable right to all the development it is capable of attaining to his fullest mental, spiritual, and physical unfolding; or, in other words, his right to PROSPER." Wallace Waddles

CONFESSION:

Through Christ, I should rule and reign as a king in this life! (Rom. 5:21) I have the power to change my feelings all of the time. My spirit rules my soul!

Out of God's glorious riches, I am strengthened with power through His Spirit in MY inner being (Eph. 3:16 NIV).

What are you really grateful for?

Every day say, "*My life is worth living well.*"

Focus

40 Days
on
Prosperity

Section #2, "About YOU"

Being Loved

Designing Your Life

Your Dreams

Your Talents

Finding Your Purpose

How Your WHYs Bring Change

Day 4 - Focus on Being Loved

Right now, do you feel unreservedly loved and cared for?

How do you know when someone loves you? What does it "feel like?"

Write about what it means to you to love someone else? How do you express love?

Write what is love to you?

The Greatest Commandment

They asked Jesus, "Teacher, which is the GREATEST commandment in the law?" Jesus replied, '"Love the Lord your God with all your heart and with all your soul and with all your mind. This is the first and greatest commandment. And the second is LIKE IT: Love your neighbor as yourself. All the laws and prophets hang on these two commandments."

1. Love God.
2. Love others.
3. Love yourself as you love others and God.

1. LOVE GOD: This is a huge topic but one that Jesus summed up when He said, "If you love me, you will do what I say" (Jn. 14:15). Loving God means that you obey the Scriptures.

2. LOVE OTHERS: The Scriptural purposes of prosperity are ultimately about loving others - social transformation brings about the reform of the Kingdom. The God kind of love confers blessings to others. With a loving state of consciousness you can transform society. This transforming love has no expectation of return.

Loving others breaks TRUE Christianity out of *just* being in the spiritual realm (Greek mentality) and includes the natural realm (the here and now). This form of loving others should be a central part of your meditation and confession. You must love others in the same way that Jesus loves you. Jesus came, died, and rose again to demonstrate the Father's love. He gave Himself up for you (Eph. 5:1-2).

> Love is the fuel for your life of success. Remember – faith works by love (Gal. 5:6).

Love Yourself

> *"I decided to love who I've been–and who I have never been. Who I am, and who I'm not... I was appreciating myself and not needing appreciation from others–"* Lizbeth Phelps

Well, the first two parts seem easy for believers. It's that last one... "love yourself" where most fail.

Most of this book will be dedicated to changing your mind-set about yourself and your surroundings.

> **You can't truly love others without FIRST loving yourself (love others AS you ALREADY love yourself).**

Most people wonder HOW God could love them at all! Especially when you know who you really are. But, if you don't love yourself, then Prosperity will be difficult. Without loving yourself, your purpose on earth can never be fully activated.

 What you believe about being genuinely, unconditionally, and eternally loved will create your belief system, your character, and your future. Understanding God's love for you is the imperative that will navigate the rest of your life toward prosperity!

Your concepts of self-love come first from your parents and environment. Your perceptions about how you were loved and treated have created a "mindset" within you. That is the main factor that formed your personality and character. Your mind-set is the expression of who you are.

- If you believe that you have to make everyone happy for them to love you, then you will just always run around trying and failing to make them happy.

- Experiences of rejection, guilt, and shame can profoundly affect you. If you think you have to conform (mind, obey) to be loved, or have to earn love by "doing" something, it will prevent you from understanding your purpose.

When you learn to love yourself, the way you relate to others will change. Your environment will change.

You are unique and one of a kind. When you realize who you are, your soul will shout, sing, and dance! Knowing you are LOVED gives you identity. It gives you hope in your future.

- God loved you when you were a sinner and still spiritually dead.

- Jesus died for you because HE loves you like you are.

- If you don't love yourself and consider yourself as blessed, then you are saying that the sacrifice of Jesus is incomplete.

The final prayer of Jesus was, "I in them and you in me. May they be brought to complete unity to let the world know that you sent me and *have loved them even as you have loved me*" (Jn. 17:23). Did you see that? God loves you as much as HE loves.... Jesus! How can you fathom that?

We must absorb the truth that Christ is IN US - -in you and me.

Our all-powerful God doesn't prefer some people more than others. In Galatians 2:6-9, Paul talks about preferential love when he discussed Peter, James and John as the pillars of the church. "*Whatever they were, it makes no difference to me; God shows personal favoritism to no one.*" God loves everyone! Out of a God of Love, all things were created. He knew you before the foundation of the world (Rev. 13:8) and He ALREADY wrote your name in the Lamb's Book of Life (Rev. 17:8). The Holy Spirit is calling you to a finished place. There is no pushing or tugging... just a call to come closer.

You may not always "feel" loved, but God simply promises that NOTHING will ever separate you from His love (Rom. 8:35-39).

God created you. You are incredibly special. Psalm 139:16 (NLT) explains that...*Every day of your life was recorded in God's book.* Every moment was laid out before a single day had passed. Notice that God has a great plan for every day of your life.

God can and will do the impossible through you,.

Loving yourself is a foundational understanding for you to obtain your full spiritual heritage.

When you love and accept yourself, it changes the way other people relate to you. You'll find a huge relationship difference as you progress in this self-love.

> The purpose
> of life
> itself is all about
> learnng to love
> and be loved!

Your beliefs, expectations, and feelings about who you are will create your world.

The greatest factor in obtaining a prosperous life, is to know without doubt that God loves you, listens to you, cares for, accepts, and connects you to Himself. His unfathomable love, and His sincere care continually reach out to fill you with Himself.

If you don't "KNOW" you're loved, you'll not be able to fully express love or properly dispense Prosperity. Loving yourself brings harmony and synchronicity to your life -- then, everything else falls into line!

Prosperity means that you intentionally align yourself with the SOURCE - which is the God of Love. Align yourself and dare to believe HIs Word!

The reason why this subject of love is early in our study is that you cannot fully focus on Kingdom prosperity until you have a revelation of already being fully accepted by God. Unworthiness, doubt, and pessimism limits the possibilities of your future.

Negative thoughts and judgments about yourself wastes energy and short circuits your success.

The primary reality that each believer must know is that the God of love dwells within. You are not God, but you can be the manifestation of God's image and likeness on this earth.

Jesus revealed His LOVE secret two thousand years ago, and it still is the only answer. If you choose to view your life as one of LOVE, you activate everything to respond back. Reciprocity is Kingdom language - you reap what you sow.

 God's purpose for you and through you is to know yourself IN CHRIST and Christ IN You. When you are secure in God's love, you can focus on your purpose!

Loving God, loving yourself, and loving others is the Great Commission of your life. We're talking about you learning to love who God has made YOU – so that you CAN fully love God and others. Only then, will you have a right motivation to be able to proceed into obtaining Biblical Prosperity!

God already loves you, He already accepts you. It is God's ultimate desire that you finish your course and be successful.

CONFESSION:
The cloud of witnesses stands on tiptoe looking over their heavenly balcony just waiting to see the astounding things I will achieve for the glory of God. I am as spiritually blessed as anyone else. I expect to prosper. The Lord wants to make me a powerful force in His Kingdom.

Love is not a state to be achieved, but a recognition of a condition. You are already loved and therefore, you are love.

Gratitude–

Understanding love opens the door to real gratitude that always heightens your awareness and clarifies what is important. Gratitude helps you CHANGE YOUR BELIEFS and restructure your mind.

Negativity is counter-productive and can take a lot of time to undo. Intentional gratefulness connects you to the Source from which the blessings come. Failure to be thankful disconnects you from the God of all POWER and all blessing.

You have already been given everything that pertains to life and Godliness. Genuine thanksgiving sends out the message that you believe that the objectives of your life are coming into reality – even before you see the answer.

Everything Matters!

Everything matters. Every little thing. Be attentive to how you respond to everyone and everything. Watch how you respond to what you already have. Yes... it's a big deal how you treat the cashier who is angry. it matters HOW you choose to express yourself concerning bad service.

The LAW OF GRATITUDE says that there is always an equal action and reaction in opposite directions. As you are thankful, you release a spiritual force that connects you to the Source of all things and obtains an instantaneous response back to you.

Notice how Jesus was always grateful, "I thank You, Father, that You hear me" (Jn. 11:41). It is gratitude that brings your whole mind into closer harmony with the creative energies of the Lord. Don't waste time thinking or talking about what should have been, the faults of the world, and the corruption of government.

What you "appreciate, appreciates."

Where can you improve in gratitude?

The key is to be grateful right now – in this moment. LIVE in genuine gratitude.

Every day say, "My life is worth living well."

Day 5 - Focus on Designing the Person You want to Be

Do you communicate doubt and unbelief about your future?

> I'm just an average person.
> I don't know how.
> I'm not good at talking to people.
> I'm quiet and shy.
> It won't work anyway - nothing ever has.
> I'll wait until next time.

Do you live and make choices because of circumstances?

Do you stop because you've never done it before (limitation)? Do you make decisions because there is no other way? Or because everyone else is doing it (consensus)? Do you make choices because there is no other way out (reaction)? Maybe you say, if this happens, then I'll do that - which allows conditions to make your decisions.

People don't respond well to those who do not know their identity. Don't expect others to belleve In you If you don't belleve in yourself. You must develop unwavering commitment to create the person you want to become. A genuine, authentic, self confident, and prosperous person.

> *"Life isn't about finding yourself. Life is about re-creating yourself."* George Bernard Shaw

Only 2% really SUCCEED - will it be you? Yes. You can beat the odds. But, you have to seriously believe that you can achieve your goals. You must work without wavering.

Remember, everything you do matters. Consistency is the key! Keep practicing and developing your new inner image (identity in Christ). You already are who God says you are... let it happen!

Loving yourself means that you replace the unproductive images of yourself - and make yourself match what the Scriptures say instead.

Let's look at your life for the major clues about what you've done right and wrong so far. RESULTS are the consequence of your past and the best forecaster of your future. Write the major results of your life so far regarding prosperity.

Write what is good about your life? What do you like?

How do you FEEL when you do something that you enjoy?

What are the landmark results of your life so far?

Hindrances

To make progress and measure it, you need to honestly assess where you are now. Can you state the truth is the way it is? If you resist facing the truth, if you deny what really is happening, you will stay frozen and static. What are the FACTS, the reality of the way it really is? See yourself in a transparent way - NOW.

Recognizing the "real you" is the beginning of seeing how to improve. Truth can really make you uncomfortable especially if you do not want to face it.

Because you are ready to see tangible results you should consider these questions:

- Do you struggle emotionally, physically, or financially right now?

- Are you looking for purpose and meaning?

- Are you in a rut?

- Have people let you down?

- Are you consistent?

- Are you motivated or look for reasons to not do what needs to be done?

- Are you confident about how you present yourself?

- Are you accountable to others?

- Do you value others? Other occupations?

- Are you planning to invade nations with Kingdom influence?

- Do you always treat people with kindness and consideration?

- Do you find taking advice difficult? Are you teachable?

- Do you tend to always find fault with others?

- Do you grow daily in self discipline?

- Are you patient?

- Are you generous?

- Do you live with integrity? Are you confidential?

- Do you bridle your tongue?

- Are you discourteous and argumentative?

- Do you work hard?

- Do you hold grudges?

- Can you keep a confidence?

- Do you waste too much time?

- Can you focus or does your mind wander? What can you do about it?

- Do you have a plan for your life? Or is it haphazard?

- Do you finish your projects?

- Do you focus on LOSS?

- Are you mentality focused inwardly (on yourself) or outwardly (on others)?
- Do you make excuses for not accomplishing things? Like what?

You have no right to complain about what you allow. Decide what belongs and what should be different in your life (Tim Byler).

Habits

90% of your daily behavior is based on your HABITS. Problems continue because they are caused by habits. A habit is a learned and acquired behavior that you do without thinking about it.

Think about it! You have everything you need to succeed. YOU are a gift to this world - and bad habits can hold you back. BAD HABITS can irritate others and even keep them from relating to you. Bad habits can cost you sales, friends, and credibility.

- Poverty thinking is a turn off.
- Being indecisive and passive - are nonproductive.
- Fighting over every offense is exhausting.
- Maybe you feel uncomfortable or intimidated. It shows.

You break habits by determination, discipline, decision, and choice. FACE the weakness and fix it. You will find breakthrough!!! Now, GO BACK and totally fill out the previous questions that you skimmed over.

What old habits, routines, and mind-sets can you surrender today?

Successful people have good habits! You want to enhance these good habits in your life. Study time, punctuality, physical fitness, nourishing diet, neatness, organization, and etc.

Say, *"My life is worth living well."*

Pray about making a list of 8 things you need to do to obtain prosperity.

Day 6 - Focus on Your Dreams

"Dream lofty dreams, as you dream, so shall you become. Your vision is the promise of what you one day shall be: your ideal is the prophecy of what you shall at last unveil." James Allen

What if you could wave a magic wand and get exactly what you have dreamed about? Shazam! Poof! It appears. Well, good things in life do not need to be an illusion.

Most everyone has dreams and they long for them to come true. But, magic won't do it, and longing isn't enough. The only way for you to bring your dreams into reality is to know without a shadow of doubt that your dreams can and should happen.

> The key to your prosperity is inside your dreams.

> Dreams captivate our imagination and show us our internal desires.

When I was in first grade, I didn't know how to ride a big two wheeler bike. But, one night I dreamed that I could ride! It was such a real dream that I woke up and went outside. Amazingly, I was able to ride that very day. There's a connection between the inner world that affects your outer world. The energy of your desire brings forth the unseen into the seen.

All of us as children had grand dreams. What were yours? Do you really know yourself and what limits you? You were conditioned as a child to think in certain ways. Ask yourself, what holds you back from seeing dreams come to pass?

Are you living out your dreams?

When did your childhood hopes end?

When were your dreams halted?

Is your dream worth living for?

"Cherish your visions and your dreams as they are the children of your soul, the blueprints of your ultimate achievements."
Napoleon Hill

Your dreams are your inner aspirations that tell you who you were created to BE. If you actualize that dream, then you find your identification and purpose.

Your dreams are a gift from God. Dare to dream BIG dreams. Even in times of great adversity, a genuine dream remains. The Great Designer of the universe planted His desire in you. He gave you the DESIRE in your heart (Ps. 37:4). Now, He wants to give you His plans as He calls you into that finished place.

Dreams express hidden desires. Desire is the urge to seek for a possible expression, or function.

The same reason a plant grows and brings forth fruit is the same reason why you grow into needing and gaining more money and wealth. Desire seeks increasing expression. You are growing. The passion to move more fully toward your destiny causes the intangible spiritual realities to come forth.

The more prosperity you have, the more God can express Himself through you.

FOCUS on remembering YOUR DREAMS: If you can't see your dreams clearly, you need to identify even the vague notions. Give detailed descriptions - dream some more about your dreams! Your dreams are intermingled with your life's purpose - God created us to *desire* what we are supposed to do!

When activated, GOD BLESSINGS can come upon your dreams. Blessings provide the things you need to express and fulfill your Divine destiny. As God's growing dunamis power in you seeks to grow and manifest, it leads to increasing internal aspirations and desires.

Allow yourself to dream again. Write about, "If my life were perfect, what would it look like?" (Talk about your tlme, resources, connections, and education.)

If someone gave you a really huge check, what would you do? Write about it.

What do you want to experience? Accomplish? Become? Contribute?

"If you can dream it, you can do it." Walt Disney

"Be intentional! LIVE YOUR DREAM!" Mark Chironna

The future belongs to those who believe in the beauty of their dreams. Eleanor Roosevelt.

What Makes You Unhappy?

"I'd rather be a flop at show business than to be a success at something I didn't lIke." George Burns

Think about the past and write down in your notebook the main things that made you unhappy, discouraged, or dissatisfied. (This could be a very long list!) Keep in mind that proper identification of a problem is the majority of the cure. Identifying your unhappiness is the first step to resolving it.

Write what makes you unhappy?

What makes you happy?

Look back over your lifetime and write what you were doing when you were the happiest? Where were you?

BEING-ness Brings Reality

BEING-ness happens as you specifically identify and move toward your purpose in life. It allows God to begin to manifest His Blessings and Goodness into His purposes for your life.

BEING-ness is an internal awareness of an external reality.

Being-ness requires that you consciously change the way you think, know, and feel about prosperity. Only with correct thinking, will your begin to experience your inner passion becoming your outer reality.

> "*Jesus touched their eyes and said, 'BECOME WHAT YOU BELIEVE.' It happened. They saw.*" (Matt. 9:27-30 MSG).

What a Statement! Become what you believe! BEING-ness! You become what you believe!

What's more... God becomes what we believe - He is Jehovah (the Ever Revealing God of Covenant). His character becomes what we need at that moment. He becomes Rapha when we are sick. He became Jireh when Abraham needed a lamb in the thicket. He is Peace in disaster.

- It is all about BEING-ness. Your God-given dreams reflect who you can become. Everything in your life will line up when you align with your true destiny.

- Your beliefs determine your actions and your actions determine your results - But first you have to believe.

- Your positive feelings and thoughts become a magnet of your God-Given desire.

 KEY: FOCUS ON THE RIGHT DREAM - that's the number one point upon which success or failure hinges.

BEING-ness determines your attitude, personality, and actions. What you believe will PROJECT into your behavior. It's the LAW OF CAUSE AND EFFECT - and this law never fails. (See Lk. 19:26). This Law is always at work - if you believe you have something, it can become yours (Mk. 11:23-24).

"The state of our physical and mental well-being is a reflection of the truth we are giving power to." –Alexander Shomlo

As you forcefully shift into your new directed mind-set toward your inner God-given desires, your conversation and demeanor changes. You take on a new way of feeling about yourself.

> Your dreams are possible. The key to seeing your God-given dreams and desires manifest, is the ability to BE and DO.

> Don't overly emphasize your situations or problems. Keep your dream alive and concentrate on the bigger picture.

> Your dreams is not what other people think you should do. Your dream is unique and won't go with the crowd.

It's your job to defend your dream, to protect it, and nurture it – no matter what. Be confident in walking out your new direction. Remember, God wants to duplicate His nature in you in order to bring you to maturity and find fulfillment in your unique and personalized life.

Make a list of the 8 dreams you want to accomplish in your life!

What I Want to Accomplish
1.
2.
3.
4.
5.
6.
7.
8.

Say, "My life is worth living well!"

Day 7 - Focus on Your Talents!

Great gifts mean great responsibilities; greater gifts, greater responsibilities! (Lk. 12:48).

Before eternity, the Lord created you to be a one-of-a-kind individual whom He could use. Psalm 130:16 says, *"Everyday of my life was recorded in your book. Every moment was (already) laid out before a single day had passed"* (NLT). Hey! That means God wrote your days and created a "GOOD" plan for your life!

TALENTS   Matthew tells us that each man was given talents *according to his own ability* (Mt. 25:15). This parable explains how two servants went out and immediately invested. But one was ruled by fear and buried his talent. You learn from this story that it is possible to lose your talents or increase your talents.

We learn from this parable that God measures and defines success differently than we do. Kingdom success requires that people faithfully develop their God-given talents and then DO what He has instructed them to do.

Everyone has some natural talents – God gave them to you. Talents are special abilities that are inborn and can increase with practice. The more you DO what you are talented to do, the better you become.

Since you didn't give yourself these talents, you don't need to take personal pride in them. However, your development of these talents plus God's empowerment is an absolute guarantee of success.

What are your greatest strengths?

- **Are you a nurturer?**
- **Are you creative?**
- **Are you spontaneous?**

What comes naturally? What do you do best? Why do people come to you?

Are you talents still buried in the ground?

What do you communicate about the most?

"A man's gifts makes room for him, and brings him before great men" **(Prov. 18:15).**

What could you do with your natural talents if you practiced?

How are you distinctive and different?

What do you want to be famous for?

What is your most valuable personal trait? When do you feel the strongest?

Your talents may conflict with what "seems to be" your abilities. Beethoven wrote his best music while he was deaf. Richard Branson (Virgin airlines) is dyslexic.

The senior crayon maker (Emerson Moser) made 1.4 billion crayons for Crayola. After he retired, he revealed that he was totally color blind! Sometimes the best accomplishments aren't naturally given, but are strengths that have grown.

Every gift and talent you increase, seeks greater expression and drives you forward to accomplish more. Be open to recognizing other people's talents and giftings and how they can fit into your life as well.

In order to learn and accomplish more, you need more prosperity. The more you achieve, the more your life expands in capacity and also desire for fulfillment.

The desire for increase is the fundamental story of the parable of the talents; only those who increase get more. Those who don't gain, have their substance taken away.

Whatever the dream is in your heart is where you must work to gain skill and strength. Doing your talents well should cause you to look forward to doing it again. Do you feel renewed and recharged? Are you fulfilled when doing it? Listen to your "*feelings*" and intuitions and catch those invigorating and energizing times.

When you are under pressure, how does your behavior affect those around you? Can they trust you? Can they count on you to deliver? [1]

If you lived your ideal life, what would you be doing in 5 years?

What IS YOUR LEGACY? What do you want others to remember about you?

Finish this statement, "When I reach the end of my life, I want to be able to joyfully remember that I did..."

---

1.   Weihenmayer, Erik, "*Summon Your Strengths.*" Success Magazine, Vol 6

- Led a healthy, happy, active life

- Enjoyed a loving spouse and family

- Fulfilled my spiritual assignments and destiny.

- Cared and helped others

BE CAUTIOUS - if you try to become too diverse or too well rounded on knowing and doing everything, you could neutralize the advantage of doing a few things well.

"Where talents and the needs of the world cross, therein lies your vocation." Aristotle

From the list of 8 things that you want to happen in your life, add how your talents fit into each one.

Make sure this list is more about what you what to do and what you need to create and manifest in your life. Be passionate about your list. What do you want to do? These are the very desires that will help you become more prosperous. (This is just to get started. You can change this as we go along.)

1.

2.

3.

4.

5.

6.

7.

8.

Do you feel gratitude for your talents?

Every day say, "My life is worth living well."

Be free to achieve your full potential. Go after everything inside yourself. Go for the whole enchilada!

"Commit your work to the Lord and then your plans will succeed" Prov. 16:3

Day 8 - Focus on Finding Purpose

F Faith activates my success
O Opportunities find me
C Consistency guarantees my success
U Understanding moves me forward
S Strategies bring results

The KEY to success is unbroken focus!

Prosperity is the FOCUS of this book - that's what we are going to talk about. Focus.

When talking about a 40 Day Focus, you need to know how to FOCUS! What is important is that you focus on the RIGHT vision and the RIGHT priorities at the RIGHT time and believe in the RIGHT results.

Know this! God is never NEED oriented. He does not (and cannot) respond to your begging and pleading. He is command controlled by your faith and follow through. God responds to your focus.

Once you decide to Focus on the RIGHT vision, all other decisions are made for you!

All studies show that successful people seem to have a common ability to laser beam focus on positive future specific goals.

People who don't succeed generally seem to have more of a "shotgun type focus" on life; they seem to be more easily distracted by too many other things - pastimes, the telephone, their e-mail, too many plans, games, excuses, or choices.

Usually, trying to do all those things that appear to be "urgent" takes you away from accomplishing what is necessary. Often, there are just too many ideas and schemes that can take you in way too many different directions.

You can never make much progress if you frequently change your mind and go a different direction.

Focus is NOW!

"The indispensable first step to getting the things you want out of life is this: Decide what you want." Ben Stein

NOW is the time to aim your life with an internal laser beam FOCUS onto prosperity. Then, you will surely see a manifestation of your goals faster as a result of this targeted focus.

Destiny is not a matter of chance; it is God given. Arriving at your destiny is a matter of personal choice – and what you decide to focus upon.

There are some fantastic universal spiritual principles about focus: What you focus on will continually develop and expand. Whatever you focus on will become your reality.

You must concentrate your focus on your pre-determined objectives. Focus on what you want to create, not what outside situations may presently exist. Your future will be determined by the thoughts and actions you decide to take. What you decide to focus on – happens...

Today you can change your relationship about money.

You must learn to FOCUS on what you can generate and bring forward. Look for new ideas, new creative ways to find success. Rise up and create your future with a determined attitude. Stop complaining about the present and focus NOW on CHANGE. Most all of us need to do some things differently. Why? Because everything is changing fast and we must integrate change in our lives. We must learn to change faster and faster!

'If you don't change your beliefs, your life will be like this forever. Is that good news?" W. Somerset Maugham

CONFESSION: *I totally reject and neutralize all unhappiness, worry, disappointment, lack, insecurity, and stress. I purpose to focus and believe in success.*

Focus on Getting God's Direction for Your Life

Our greatest fear is not that we are inadequate, but that we are powerful beyond measure.

Today is an important day. You must discover the powerful purpose for your life. This purpose will become your vision. The exercises in this book will help you develop this vision. Once you know what you should do, everything else falls into line!

- Set aside some time to hear from God about the prosperity of your future.

- Make it your business to get Divine direction.

- WRITE IT DOWN. You need to develop a clarified direction (vision) and then fix your mind on that ONE vision. Let all your feelings, thoughts, and behaviors be supportive toward that vision.

- Pray, declare, and confess about gaining true prosperity in your life.

- Make a total commitment to stay focused on your vision to prosper.

- Once you hear from God, keep your intention focused. Stop struggling. Know that God will do what He has promised. Have faith. Find His vision and DO IT - then stand.

God's desire for you must become your focal intention. Be unwavering, unmoved, and un-discouraged! Don't take your mind off of it. Don't give up! Don't deviate or change your mind. Be indomitable. Be intentionally conscious of your direction every minute of every day.

"Any enterprise is built by wise planning, becomes strong through common sense, and profits wonderfully by keeping abreast of the facts" (Prov. 24:3-6).

Believe and know with unwavering conviction that your promised future is already yours. That means... act like it is yours. Talk like it's already in existence. Take ownership of it! Use it. Hold it. Live in this realm of FAITH until it makes an appearance (Heb. 11:1).

Caution

My friend, PROSPERITY WON'T JUST FALL INTO YOUR LAP just because you are a nice person! This is almost an impossible statement to accept. But, you can pray for forty years for things to happen, you can stand in faith, and make the right confessions - and still nothing happens.

Many people have had true prophetic words that have not come to pass. That is always because they need to align to their true purpose in life and then DO something that corresponds to that word.

 If you ever listen to anything, this is it! Get the mind of God for your life and THEN – BE IT and GO DO IT!

Action is required (James 2:26). Finish this book and enact your God-given vision! Today deliberately choose to affirm how you want to build and LIVE YOUR LIFE.

If you can't do what you planned, then DO something. Don't just sit there and wait! Go sweep the floor, buy the computer program you need, wash the car, or do something.

Nobody follows a parked car. Stop waiting for the ice cream truck to come and drop dollars into your lap. The Holy Spirit isn't Tinkerbell continuously bringing your Krispy Kream doughnuts of prosperity. Do something.

When Paul was on his way to Macedonia, the Spirit turned him a different direction. Get moving and allow God to speak.

Everything you need is waiting for you to align your thoughts and get ready.

Know that you have the ability to "do it" no matter what the circumstances. You can experience unlimited life. Prosperity helps provide you with freedom and choices.

Begin with the End in Mind

God has ordained you to be THE ARCHITECT OF YOUR OWN LIFE.

This ONE thing is now a picture of your VISION. God is committed to His promises.

- Focus on the Scriptures that are necessary for you to achieve your vision.

- Focus on how to spend 80% of your time.

- Focus on specific objectives that pertain to the specific areas in your life. Don't have generalized concepts.

- Don't allow someone else to set your goals for you. Take ownership of your life.

- Focus on NOT wasting time by procrastinating.

- Believe that you receive the promises NOW.

- Duplicate YOUR focus and find solutions to problems.

- Focus on daily driving forward to destiny and productivity.

- Focus on what YOU can do that no one else can do.

- Continue being flexible and proactive.

"The minute you choose to do what you really want to do it's a different kind of life." R. Buckminster Fuller

"Have the courage of being your genuine self, of standing alone and not wanting to be somebody else." – Yutang

"The minute you choose to do what you really want to do it's a different kind of life." R. Buckminster Fuller

Day 9 - Focus on the WHYs of Change

"No man is a failure who is enjoying life." William Feather

WHY do you want success and prosperity? Some people answer: To be my own boss, to feed the poor, to optimize my life, or to sleep in. Others say to provide for my family, to enhance my quality of life, or to live a LIFE that benefits others. To travel or preach for generations to come! How about, to LIVE a quickened life and to share that life with my children and grandchildren?

Your answers to these "why questions" are you MOTIVES. You want to know why you are doing things because when you *really* have a great WHY, you won't quit. It is important to invest time in knowing WHY.

What are the top reasons WHY you want success?

An important WHY supplies the energy, passion, and the momentum you need to keep going until you win. Winners stay committed as long as it takes. Once you set your life's course, a WHY will move you forward.

Obstacles will always come! You must decide now (before uncertainties happen) to never quit! Your WHY will keep you from quitting! Just praying isn't enough - you have to finish your course. A list of powerful WHYs (motive) will re-activate you!

Endurance will outweigh all natural will power! Fortitude maintains your forward momentum. Remember the turtle race - it doesn't really matter how slow you go - just don't quit!

Go back to your list of 8 important things you want to accomplish, and write the WHYs that will cause you to win.

In your notebook, draw a picture of your WHYS. (Seriously.) Or cut out pictures in magazines. Put the picture where you can see it every day!

Trace that photo with your fingers

Meditate daily on your WHYs.

WHY? Whys are about possessing what is yours to have. WHYS keep you on course. As they said in Apollo 13: "Failure is not an option."

Biblical Mindset

The nation of Israel had some incredible promises about prosperity (for example, Deuteronomy 28:9-13). But, we know that they never apprehended the promises.

Israel was caught up with unbelief, excuses, and fear that kept them from acquiring the things that the Lord God wanted to give them. Their promises went UNCLAIMED! Finally, Obadiah prophesied that Israel would change and *fully possess its own possessions* (Obd. 17).

Most believers have not fully possessed the promises of God. Hopefully, you have learned your WHYs. Now work on building your faith so that the promises can be yours!

Faith is the conduit that connects the spiritual to the temporal realm.

It's not about having it all together or doing things perfectly - it's about the faith and determination to possess your possessions!

Faith is the victory born of God that overcomes the world (1 Jn. 5:4). Faith IS the victory. It is because of our FAITH that we overcome. FAITH brings what is needed. God is looking for FAITH.

"Have two goals: Have the right God kind of faith and the wisdom - that is, knowing and doing right. Don't let them slip away, for

they fill you with living energy and bring you honor and respect"
(from Prov. 3:21-22).

CONFESSON: *I walk by unwavering faith and expectation relying entirely on God's ability to bring me to my destiny. I joyfully do what I never imagined I could do.*

WHYs Focus on Your Future

"If at first the idea is not absurd, then there is no hope for it."
Albert Einstein

If God gives you your dream, then you can do it. Unless you want to be a roller derby star and have a serious physical disability (or something like that), you CAN do it! With God, all things are possible. No boundaries and no restrictions can stop you.

WHYs give you the persistence to consciously design your life. That means you can remove the limits on your life by liberating your mind! This renewal is a continuous process. YOU can cause your life to work for you if you embrace change and learn to make your thoughts work for you.

Whatever is truly God's intention for you will manifest itself through you when you determine what it is and how to get there.

Write down – "What can God do through me?"

Write an affirmation about WHY you want to re-create your life!

Say, "My life is worth living well."

Your purpose is to help establish the Kingdom of God in this earth!

40 Days on Prosperity

Section #3, "Your Attitude"

Excuses

Overcoming

Attitudes

Thoughts and Words

Abundance

Winning

Day 10 - Focus on No More Excuses

"Excuses are the nails used to build a house of failure."
Don Wilder and Bill Rechin

EXCUSES. - An excuse is a lie. It keeps you from accepting responsibility or from acting and saying "yes." An excuse justifies doing what you want to do. It is a false belief that you make up to keep from doing something else. Excuses hold you in mediocrity.

Excuses cause you to fall short of your destiny. No excuse is ever worth the time to tell it!

YOU MUST REVEAL YOUR EXCUSES TO YOURSELF! Why do you settle for less than your dream? What limits your ability? It is time to find about what you must do to achieve prosperity.

"If you don't want to do something, one excuse is as good as another." Yiddish Proverb

A great opportunity can pass by – all because you're made an excuse. Maybe they won't understand. You're too busy. It's not the right time. You're quiet and shy. Afraid. Not good at talking to people. Don't like to drive. Want to wait till next time. It won't work anyway...

Is your main hope for success - the lottery?

- Excuses keep you in poverty.
- Where did this epidemic of excuses to keep you in poverty start?
- They keep you looking for "luck and good fortune."

- They create an irresponsible mind-set that easily turns to deficiency.

- Do you recognize the mind-sets that shape your life and expectations of success?

- When were those lies whispered into your ear?

Accurate acknowledgement about what has hindered you in the past will bring a quick shift of perception and further transformation. It's time to experience the reality of knowing who you are and the excuses you use.

What are your excuses for not being a success?

(I.E. #1, I wish I had time to pray, write a book, etc. But I can't because....)

Where do you see yourself in five years?

How do you spend your money right now?

Do you have any regrets about money?

Write about how your attitudes about prosperity will affect your future, your kid's future and your grandchildren's future?

"...You will have to give up blaming and complaining and take TOTAL responsibility for your life–that means all your results, successes and failures...if you realize that (no matter how bad, hard, or difficult it has been) YOU created your current conditions, you can un-create them and recreate them at will..."
Authur Clement Stone

Biblical Mindset

"There are a thousand excuses for every failure but never a good reason." Mark Twain

Excuses began with the first sin ever committed. The Lord asked Adam, "Have you eaten from the tree that I commanded you not to eat from?" The man's excuse was the woman. He said, "The woman you put here with me—she gave me some fruit from the tree, and I ate it." Then the Lord God said to the woman, "What is this you have done? The woman excused herself by saying, "The serpent deceived me, and I ate."(Gen. 3:11-13, NIV).

One great consequence of the Fall was making excuses. Here are some more Scriptures about making excuses.

Someone else made me do it!
> Adam and Eve: Genesis 3: 12-13
> Aaron: Exodus 32: 22-24
> Moses: Numbers 20: 10-12, Deut 3: 25-27
> Saul: 1Samuel 15:20-21

I can't do it!
> Moses: Exodus 4:10
> Children of Israel: Numbers 13:31-14:4
> Gideon: Judges 6:15

I'm too busy!
> Luke 9: 59-62 - wanting to bury their father.
> Luke 14: 18-20 - take care of land, ox, and wife.
> Acts 24: 24-25 - Felix

YOU are the Only Answer

 Who do you think really stops you from living your dream? Truthfully, there is nothing stopping you, but YOU.

Your excuses are the biggest obstacle to successful prosperity! That limited mind-set is your worst enemy. The biggest Goliath you will ever fight is that person you see in the mirror!

- You need to take total responsibility for where you are now.

- Don't allow other people or circumstances to limit your beliefs any longer.

- It's time to change your MIND and your thoughts.

- Only YOU can limit yourself from this day forward.

Remember this

It's not about *trying;* It's about KNOWING it will work. If you don't believe that you can do it – you probably won't.

Excuses waste time. Benjamin Franklin said, *"Remember that time is money."* Don't allow excuses, distractions, or uncertainty to rob you. Convince your brain that what you do will succeed. Prophesy to yourself the Word of the Lord. The stronger you are convinced about your success, the faster you move forward.

Eliminating your excuses corrects your attitude! The right mindset opens up the flow of God's Gifts into your life. Your attitude determines your opportunities and your success. You are what you are and where you are because of your thinking. Cause always equals effect.

"...Look within and find God! God closes doors no man can open and God opens doors no man can close. If you need God to open some doors for you... just look within." Dennis Carpenter

Today is the day to take 100% responsibility for your life. You must stop settling for things as they are, and develop the crucial conviction that success is achievable and imperative. Be fervently convinced! Face each day ready to solve problems and to lead.

The greatest failure is not believing.

Excuses cause people to quit or not to stick with things long enough. But, life waits to bring you a breakthrough. You can find spontaneous results any time you become open to apprehend them.

Perhaps it's time to decide that you were put on earth to make a difference! If it isn't you who will do it, then who?

The good news is that you can EXCEED every expectation! You can change your personal outlook, your health, yourself, and your surroundings. You can begin to EXPECT the best!

CONFESSION: *"I am responsible for my success. I take ownership of my future. Right now I receive inspired ideas and defined direction. I appreciate the talents and abilities that God has given and I will use them to take action and achieve the fulfillment of my God given destiny."*

After getting rid of excuses, list the ACTUAL obstacles (and people) that really stand in your way

List the main things that keep you from optimum success. Then, order this list in priority. The number one item will be the first thing for you to conquer. These obstacles may be external (financial, lack of education) or internal (attitude, concepts). You may need to use more paper!

What belief systems and attitudes do you need to change to have the success you want?

What are you really grateful for?

.

Work on refining and DOING your list!

Every day say, *"My life is worth living well."*

Day 11 - Focus on Overcoming Discouragement:

'History has demonstrated that the most notable winners usually encountered heartbreaking obstacles before they triumphed. They won because they refused to become discouraged by their defeats.' –B. C. Forbes

It is said by some that 98% of all believers have had their hopes of success dashed - in nearly every area of their lives. Discouragement and dullness fogs the lens of their future vision.

Does discouragement and rejection stand between you and YOUR SUCCESS story?_____

Discouragement is the quickest way to failure!

So... what causes you to be discouraged and fail?

What keeps you up at night?

You can't change what you are willing to tolerate!

Sometimes you may not be able to live up to someone's expectations or do what they have asked. Their disappointment can cause a self-rejection in you.

Rejection:	David was a great Israelite warrior in King Saul's army. One day, Saul heard the accolades about David as the town's women danced and sang: "'*Saul has slain his thousands, and David his tens of thousands*' "(1 Sam. 18:7).

Saul felt rejected and discouraged when he said, *"They have credited David with tens of thousands,"* he thought, *"but me with only thousands. What more can he get but the kingdom?"* (1 Sam. 18:8)

After saying this, Saul could never lead correctly. Insecurities, jealousy, and fear caused him to strive for more control. His anger escalated every time he heard about another one of David's successes. Soon, Saul wanted to kill David at every opportunity.

Saul could have viewed David as an invaluable part of his team but he looked at him as a threat.

You may be experiencing rejection right now. But, look again... IF things are not like you need them to be, it's up to you to expect prosperous ideas to come into your life. There is no time for self pity.

Learn how to deal with rejection. Be mentally tough.

- Rejection is inevitable. It will happen again.

- You will not be nor can you be everyone's perfect person.

- Nobody can steal your talents or skills.

- You must learn to handle working with imperfect people.

- Enduring rejection develops character.

- Are they rejecting you or the product? You or the choice you offer?

Jeremiah	What is success to you? Does it require that everyone likes you? Do you need approval for everything you do? Is it never being rejected? By these standards, Jeremiah was a miserable failure. For 40 years (not days) he served as God's prophet to the tribe of Judah, but when Jeremiah spoke, nobody listened.

Again we see how the Lord intended to bless Israel, but they couldn't receive it. Nobody listened to what Jeremiah said. He went through severe deprivation to deliver his messages: He was thrown into prison (chap. 37), thrown into a cistern (chap. 38), and forcibly taken to Egypt against his will (chapter 43). He was rejected by the kings (36:23), his neighbors (11:19-21), his family (12:6), the false priests and prophets (20:1, 2; 28:1-17), friends (20:10), and those who heard him (26:8). Yet he didn't stop.

Throughout his life, Jeremiah was rejected. He stood alone, declaring God's promises as he wept over the fate of his beloved country.

When your times get rough, remember Jeremiah. He spoke truth and no one listened. In the eyes of those around, Jeremiah was not a success. But, to the Lord, Jeremiah was one of the most successful people of all time.

Godly success involves agreement with God's intention and His unswerving faithfulness. Regardless of resistance and persecution, Jeremiah faithfully continued out his life in obedience to his calling.

It was during these most difficult times that Jeremiah wrote, "'For I know the plans I have for you,' declares the Lord, 'Plans to prosper you and not to harm you, plans to give you hope and a future" (Jer. 29:11). It is time to ask yourself if you can you receive His PLAN for your life? Even in times of difficulty, can you enter into the plans that will PROSPER you and give you future hope?

> **"Believe in the Lord your God, and you shall be established; believe His prophets, and you shall PROSPER (2 Chron. 20:20).**

Fear   Your subconscious doesn't discern any difference between reality and your imagination. Both can equally produce anxiety, concern, worry, fear, and emotional and physical reactions. Feeling rejected can be real or imaginary.

- Rejection can be your biggest hindrance to success. Sorrowfulness will use your soul (mind, will, and emotions – heart) to create what you DON'T WANT.

- What you believe will happen – good or bad (Job 3:25).

"Focus on where you want to go, not on what you fear."
Anthony Robbins

"Too many people let others stand in their way and don't go back for one more try." Rosabeth Moss Kanter

"We only become what we are by the radical and deep-seated refusal of accepting that which others have made up."
–Jean-Paul Sartre

Everyone fails sometimes. Failure can be viewed as a temporary condition on your way to success. What you need to know is how to sometimes anticipate failure and learn how to keep it from happening again.

Great derailment happens if you allow the outside world to determine your internal outlook. And vice versa – If your are disappointed internally, then your external world will also mirror this disappointment. Disappointment and unforgiveness actually dulls your appearance. There will be a foggy indistinctness about your reactions. Connecting with other people will be difficult.

Someone else's opinion of you should not become your reality!

You can't fully prosper if you feel rejected or demeaned. You need to overcome these emotions (like rejection, discouragement, and fear) today.

Everyone has horrible events happen to them. Some will betray you. Some will disappoint you. You must learn to handle problems in mature ways - it's okay to experience sadness - but don't be a victim. Bad things will happen but you can learn to cope with them. Gain greater skills to handle problems.

The best way to control negative emotions is simply to command your mind to stop dwelling on them and purposefully FOCUS on what has been given you to control.

Negative thoughts about others will hinder you, waste your time, and keep you from moving forward.

Everyone has setbacks. But you must teach your soul to focus on right goals and not the potential bad things that happen. You must become resilient and able to bounce back stronger after each setback. You must get back up every time you fall!

What has significantly disappointed you in the past?

Who do you need to forgive in order to move on?

"When one door closes, another opens. But we often look so regretfully upon the closed door that we don't see the one that has opened for us." – Alexander Graham Bell

> Negative thoughts about others will hinder you, waste your time, and keep you from moving forward.

When something bad happens again, just remember that you aren't going there anymore. Remember that what happened last year can't be changed. But, every past experience should have taught you valuable information. You must learn to view those past experiences as opportunities to learn.

Biblical Mindset

Jesus was despised and rejected above all others. He endured rejection so that you don't have to. To take up this rejection after He died to take it away is a serious fault. Anything that prevents you from living in total victory can become a continual offense to the Finished Work of the cross, and could cause you to not see the success you need.

When merely surviving hurts and disappointments are no longer enough - you must move forward. It is not time to withdraw, it is time to press into apprehending the finished work.

Let the past be past at last! Don't keep struggling in these areas of your soul. Believe God to help you to not be victimized by your emotional disappointments any longer. Let go of the past (Phil. 3:13-14).

You will never make everyone happy. Don't let that disappoint you ever again.

"I don't know the key to success, but the key to failure is trying to please everybody." Bill Cosby

"Nobody grows old by merely living a number of years. People grow old by deserting their ideals. You are as young as your faith, as old as your doubt; as young as your self confidence, as old as your fear; as young as your hope, as old as your despair."
General Douglas MacArthur

FORGIVENESS causes a release and a new beginning in your life. You will suddenly feel better, more aware, sleep better, and enjoy life. Forgiveness activates the **ENERGY** to eliminate discouragement and disappointment. You must learn to quickly forgive and bless those who offend you...

CONFESSION: *My circumstances DO NOT MAKE MY CHOICES for me! I don't get upset or mad about the small stuff! I have control over my emotions. I can not be offended. I don't look back. I do not regard a wrong. I forget the past and press to the high calling!*

I know how to dream BIG and even BIGGER. My future is much more exciting and fun than my past. "Who I am is what fulfills me and fulfills the vision I have of the world."

What are you grateful for?

Work on **DOING** your list!

Every day say, *"My life is worth living well.*

Day 12 - Focus on a Prosperous Attitude

Unfortunately, a poverty mind-set still sweeps much of the Church. The concept of intentional blessing of prosperity has been weakened and lost!

We must find accurate revelation beyond the past extreme teachings of both poverty teachings and the manipulative teachings.

It is vital that we communicate new relevance and discover what the original language of the Bible actually says about having money. We must see past Hellenistic thinking and understand that God wants us to influence our world. Also, we must love ourselves in order to inherit our promises!

We discussed in earlier chapters about the Hebrew worldview that understood the co-existence of the spiritual and the natural. The Greeks considered only the spiritual realm as important.

Do you know that you have been highly influenced by Greek thought? And... do you know that your relationship to Scriptures as they relate to prosperity are most likely founded in Greek influence on Western Culture and education, rather than the intention of God?

Unfortunately, religious mentalities continue to try and stop you from success. Be assured that it is NOT more holy or more noble to live and deny your mind, deny your soul, or deny your body. We are supposed to integrate ourselves and co-exist in both the spiritual and the natural worlds.

It does not make you closer to God to be poor or sick. If you live in unexpressed potential or function, you will be unhappy. Your God given goals require money to accomplish them. It is absolutely Scriptural that you would want to have money and prosperity.

 You must totally get rid of any trace of the notion that there is or may be any force in the universe - or any poverty minded deity who wants to keep you poor, or who is able to make you poor, or whose objectives could possibly be served by keeping you in poverty.

God Shows Up In This World!

The correct Biblical worldview is for the church and believers to affect BOTH the tangible and intangible realms. The very first thing Jesus said in His first public address in a synagogue was to preach the gospel to the poor (Lk. 4:18). This was the first thing on His mind. Social transformation should have primary focus in our churches.

The Bible is written with this intention of no divisions between natural and spiritual. Jesus and every Bible author believed this way.

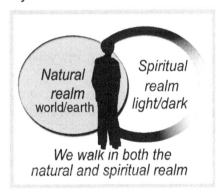

Natural realm world/earth

Spiritual realm light/dark

We walk in both the natural and spiritual realm

Remember our earlier discussion about Hebrew thought verses Greek thought. Hebrew thought shows us now to co-exist in the natural and the Spiritual at the same time.

In order for Spiritual prosperity to work for you, you have to walk in both the natural and the spiritual at the same time. This co-existing can be called being spirit/souled![1] This means that the Kingdom of God begins to exist in your temporal life.

---

1. See my book "Connecting" for in depth study of co-existing.

The spiritual ALWAYS manifests in the temporal. When God blesses us spiritually, IT IS ALWAYS OBVIOUS AND SEEN! God wants to BLESS His people.

We now know that the spirit and the natural must not be viewed as two distinct segments of life. We are spirit/souled in order to walk on this earth as a human being imbued by/with God in order to impact this world with the Kingdom.

Truth teaches us to receive the promises and inheritance of God here on earth - NOW, in this lifetime.

You must be totally convinced that Jesus is THE GIFT from God and that salvation gives you an inward experience of fellowship with the Lord that results in the transformation of every external aspect of your life.

In whatever sphere or circumstance God has placed you, when your motives are right, you may seek to prosper within those specific areas.

Today we have access to more accurate meanings of the original words used in Scriptures. And from this we KNOW that abundance and prosperity are really truths that not many believers have used accurately. We must learn truth and then apply it.

Prosperity is a Blessing!

'It pleases the Lord to make you PROSPER" (Deut. 28:63).

 True prosperity is the fullness of everything you need in life to fulfill your destiny. Health, wealth, balance, authority, and WHOLENESS in your spirit, soul, and body. Prosperity is what we all need. Prosperity is totality and abundance in your finances as well as your entire life. Prosperity includes your time, health, and energized relationships with people you love. It is how we share the Gospel and help others.

Money can be transient while prosperity is a lifetime treasure. Money is not necessarily synonymous with success. But, having abundant prosperity is true success!

"Prosperity is living easily and happily in the real world, whether you have money or not!" Jerry Gellis

Prosperity is an Attitude

"The man who acquires the ability to take full possession of his own mind may take possession of anything else to which he is justly entitled." Andrew Carnegie

A wrong attitude can cause you to live BY DEFAULT. A person can intellectually understand about right principles and not genuinely trust in the God of love and prosperity! That really says that to you, that there is no such thing.

Right decisions attract Godly responses in your life. It's time to MANAGE YOUR LIFE! You must identify wrong beliefs that govern and create your life.

Your mind-set, theological presuppositions, and circumstances regarding money are probably the same as they've been for a long time. If you say, "I can't afford that!" Then you probably have said that for many years. It has become an attitude.

What is your internal picture of Prosperity? Close your eyes and pretend that money is a person (man or woman) who is standing in front of you. This is just an exercise - don't worry. Take time to see what this "person" looks like. Is it illusive and cruel? Tormenting and taunting. Is he tall and angry with his arms crossed? Old with a beard? Describe what you see...

It's time to see money as kind. Cause your image of this "person" to be one who gives you approval. Begin to create a "new person." One who loves you and relates to you in ever giving generosity. Visualize prosperity uncross his arms and hold out his hands to you.

Believe that the Lord wants to bring you finances to you that will help you reach your destiny!

 "A successful attitude can be defined as the progressive achievement of a worthy ideal, or objective." Success is a progressive application of

right decisions. Gaining an attitude of prosperity and success in life generates happiness and motivation

Science now is beginning to show that the right ATTITUDE is paramount to success! You can see that Truth in Scriptures. Look at these translations of Ephesians 4:23,

"...Be made new in the attitude of (your) minds" (4:23, NIV).

"Your attitudes and thoughts must all be constantly changing for the better" (4:23, AMP).

"And be constantly renewed in the spirit of your mind (having a fresh mental and spiritual attitude" (Eph. 4:24).

Your Attitude Determines Your Success Or Failure

Abundance involves transforming the poverty attitude of your "old man" that traps you at your current level of success -- into the NEW man. You actually ADVANCE into the next level!

- Your attitude is determined by your BELIEFS, choices, values, thoughts, expectations, and culture.

- Your attitude can change your future.

- The RIGHT attitude will pole vault you into the NEXT LEVEL of your own full potential.

The inheritance of the upright shall be forever. (Ps. 37:18)

The revenue of the Spirit can transform you! Like we said earlier, the Lord *already* blesses you with every heavenly and earthly blessings. You already have ALL THINGS that pertain to life and godliness, prosperity of soul and health of body (2 Pet. 1:3, 3 Jn. 1:2).

CONFESSION: "I have decided to receive God's love and prosperity by Faith. God supplies all my need according to His riches in glory (Phil. 4:19), therefore, all lack is removed from my life. Prosperity, overflows into my life. It pours into my family and my church. Prosperity finds me and overtakes me with blessings (Deut. 28:2)!"

Day 13 - Focus on Prosperous Thoughts & Words!

"Never say anything about yourself you do not want to come true." - Brian Tracy

Gaining wealth has certain laws that you must to follow. There are natural laws -- just like gravity is a natural law, we know that there are spiritual laws of prosperity. Prosperity is not just the result of saving money or being smart about it. It's not selecting the right business niche or having enough capital (you can get that). Or just having the right marketing plan...

 There is one principle that is demanded for you to know -- Your thoughts and words can and will bring forth tangible wealth from nothingness. Thoughts and words produce reality.

Said another way, bad thoughts and words can never produce good results and good thoughts and words will never produce bad results.

Jesus said, "Therefore I tell you, whatever you ask for in prayer, believe that you HAVE (*already*) received it, and it will be yours" (Mk. 11:24). This means you act like and talk like it has already happened!

Nature is the visible expression of God's thoughts and words. His words created the motion of energy to create a mountain, a sheep, and a human. Our world is a world of creative thoughts and words. In fact, YOU are a word!

Thoughts with correct words create the vehicle for the Holy Spirit (God's energy) to work - you cannot bring something to pass until you have thought it and spoken it. Humanity was created to create what he/she thinks and speaks. You are a creator.

Begin to Scripturally verbalize your Godly purpose, it will happen. Just speak what is already yours. *"it is your Father's pleasure to give you the kingdom."* Jesus said it!

Thoughts

You are the sum total of your experiences and anything you've allowed into your mind to influence you.

From the time you were born, inputs have come into your soul. From the way you were held, to the music you heard, the books you've read, the people you've known.

Your future is created by your thoughts. If you are not in control of your thoughts, it means you have allowed random thoughts by other people to create your future for you. You must take charge of your own mind in order to accomplish God's plan for your destiny.

Your senses are gates of entry that influence you. That's why we need to be cautious about what we watch, what we listen to, what we read. Everything has an influence.

My friend, your only limitations are: 1) your perception of who God is and 2) your perception of who God is IN YOU. God is bigger than you think!

"The mind is the limit. As long as the mind can envision the fact that you can do something, you can do it."
Arnold Schwarzenegger

What you BELIEVE (focus on) in your mind (soul, heart, inner world) creates your reality (outer world). Proverbs says, *"As a man (person) thinks in his HEART (soul), so he is"* (23:7).

Your mental and emotional thoughts determine your outer world.

The heart is really about feelings. You need to remain conscious of focusing your optimistic *feelings* about prosperity in order to begin to generate the experiences you want. Choose to maintain and keep positive feelings and thoughts for out of your heart are the *"issues of life"* (Prov. 4:23).

Your mind has certain creative properties. Do you see what you think about always happens? Good or bad?

Everything you permit to dwell in your mind (heart, soul) will influence your future. As you think in your heart, you become!

- Your mind thinks about what it is exposed to.
- Exposure shapes your perception. What your read, hear (the music you play and your conversation), and even your daydreams all shape who YOU ARE.

Scripture shows us that what you fear will happen (Job 3:25). Focusing on what is negative will surely cause more bad things to happen! Negative thoughts and ideas result in discouragement and unclear (unfocused) activities.

You have three kinds of thoughts:

- Those you create yourself.
- Those that respond to your circumstances.
- Those that come from what you learn.

You have two kinds of mentality. There's the 1) BUDGET MENTALITY that tries to make everything work through small details and tight reigns. Then, there's the 2) VISION MENTALITY that looks at what needs to be accomplished, considers the cost, and decides to do what is necessary to make it happen.

Unproductive people live in a static world without hope. Limiting beliefs and words often hold them back. If someone believes that they are too old to work anymore and that they won't have a job for long – then, no matter how well they function in that job, their reality of expectation will come to pass in the real world. Soon, their job will be given to another.

Addictive negative words and thoughts brings catastrophic results. Poverty mindedness and laziness take a toll on our future.

If you say, "It's going to be really hard," then your actions will align with those feelings of being overwhelmed, "I can't do it." Then, of course, you can't do it! Internal RESISTANCE will continue until you STOP your negative thoughts. You must recognize and identify this resistance and speak into it with correct words.

Everything that you allow into your mind influences your life.

All your thoughts can be brought into your direct control. You can take control of your thoughts anytime you decide to do it! Command your mind to agree with the Word of God!

Remember, Jesus said in Matthew 9:29, "According to your faith, so be it unto you!" We mentioned earlier the Scripture in Proverbs 23:7, "As a man *thinks* in his heart, so is he!" Thoughts create our personality, or sense of being.

Lots of believers fail to enjoy their lives. They are filled with negative and self-defeating messages like, "I hate my job, I hate doing this." "I can't do this!" "Why should I do it?" "Who cares?"

Uncertain sounds

These uncertain sounds (1 Cor. 14:8) (words) actually program and pre-frame your brain -- and you are not able to be motivated to do a decent job! Why not enjoy life and have fun? Try giving your subconscious more empowering messages.

We discover that God used empowering WORDS to create and enlighten the world. "Let there BE light!" Words matter - even those that you say to yourself and under your breath.

What is the internal conversation that you have with yourself? Do you use words like, "But, maybe, when I have the time, I can't, and it's too difficult?" Or do you use words like, "Achieve, complete, possibility, accomplish, and catapulting! I CAN DO IT!" Say the words and act like you can do it!

"Believe, act the part, and say the words to become it!"

Remember this

Deliberately set your concentration and attentiveness on being radiantly successful in your spirit, soul, and body. Determine to be free of powerlessness. Meditate on the Goodness of the Living God and rest in knowing that He chose you to be alive in this moment in time. True prosperity originates from the Divine Source of your life.

"Your ears must hear your mouth talk like God!" Cathy Walker

Using God's Words becomes the bridge between this earth and the power of God being manifested in the physical realm. This is really important, so don't just skim over this part.

Right WORDS change your future. Today (and every day) try to speak only positively about how you feel, what you desire, and what you expect.

Words create impressions, imagery, and expectations - either positive or negative. Words build powerful neurological pathways that actually influence and change how we think. There's an astonishing relationship between the words we use and the results we get.

If you can't trust what you say, how will you believe what God says?

You can change your Words!

Commit yourself to proactive behavior and determine with absolute certainty to use the correct words that can and will influence your success and health. Correct words create your consciousness.

Godly thoughts and expressions produce the power that underlies every action and event in the world.

77

Think about the importance of using the right words. Consider the choice between "spend" and "invest." Do you want to find a bank that will spend your money or invest it? Since spending usually means taking away your money – you probably would prefer a bank that invests.

Poorly chosen words can kill your own expectation and negatively impact everything in your life. Words influence the people in your life. In order to achieve anything great, you must gain mastery and self control over both your thoughts and words.

You've probably heard about the power of words before. It is easy to think you understand this point, but it can be the most difficult process to master.

> **If you want to prosper, learn to harness the power of your words.**

Want better results? Check your words.

THE GREATEST SABOTAGE of all is when you are not true to yourself. You cannot control your external environment - but YOU CAN (by your will) control your words, thoughts, and actions.

Change your conversation and you CAN alter the trajectory of your entire future.

Words are seeds of faith in your soul. Negative words can kill your dreams. Thousands of research studies that prove the astoundingly benefits of positive words. Great power is available to you if you remember this: *"The power of life and death is in the tongue"* (Prov. 18:21).

With patient practice, you will find yourself moving toward your desired outcome! You must "Walk the talk." Do what you say. Your words must become your actions. All your vision, goals, hopes and dreams are irrelevant if you don't talk right. YOUR WORDS lead to success.

Remember, you are a self-fulfilling prophecy. It's time to commit to optimize your life.

Write here about how your choice of words helps you obtain Kingdom Success.

"Everything we say signifies; everything counts, that we put out into the world. It impacts on kids, it impacts on the zeitgeist of the time." Meryl Streep

Build your own strong personal confession that is consistent with how you need to think about money according to your true dreams and goals.

Along with your own confession, add this CONFESSION:
The Kingdom is already here (Mat. 4:17) and I will walk in it! My thoughts and words create my life. I communicate on a Kingdom level.

All things are possible for me. Outrageous prosperity and wholeness are already created and finished for me. My spirit, soul, and body are transformed into achieving abundant living (zoe). I can walk in this specific area of faith because I already please God (Heb. 11:6). God rewards me with victory. I'm not worried or anxious. I don't fear inability, or poverty, or failure. That which I set my hand to will prosper.

"It's time to start living the life you've imagined" - Henry James

Review the list of 8 things you want to accomplish, and re-write the words in more powerful faith-filled terms and use positive action verbs (not passive tense). State in first person, "I am..."

1
2
3
4
5
6
7
8

"In her (Wisdom's) left hand are RICHES and honor" (Prov. 3:16).

Day 14 - Focus on Abundance

Jesus said, *"The thief comes only to steal, kill, and destroy, but I came that you may have life and have LIFE more ABUNDANTLY"* (Jn. 10:10). Jesus came to give us ABUNDANT life -- but not every believer finds abundant life.

Right now, is your life ABUNDANT?

- Do you believe that there is enough resources for everyone?
- Do you focus on what you don't have? That you LACK?
- Do you really enjoy your LIFE? (Be honest!)
- Do you want to fully experience abundant *(zoe)* LIFE?

"I could not, at any age, be content to take my place by the fireside and simply look on. Life was meant to be lived. Curiosity must be kept alive. One must never, for whatever reason, turn his back on life." —Eleanor Roosevelt(1884-1962)

Abundance isn't found by just having lots of things and extra cash. It isn't found by endless endeavors. Godly prosperity is not about having too many fancy cars and being able to drop important names. Prosperity is not about greed, or selfish ambition, or just having lots of possessions (Luke 12:15). It is about enjoying abundance and having what you need to enjoy life and help others.

The abundance of prosperity is all about making your life right, achieving your destiny, helping others, and leaving a legacy for your family and the world

There's enough for you. Abundance is everywhere – gold has not left the earth. Money is still around. It just needs to trade places.

The Blessing of God is abundance (see Deut. 18) and the rule of the Scriptures is ever expanding abundance. Everything of God is always increasing. Since you can gain what you Divinely imagine and internally conceive, it is time to allow it to GROW and increase?

Abundant thinking allows you to have opportunities that come to fulfill your destiny. The ABUNDANT Law of Scripture says there is MORE than enough for everyone.

Jesus Desires to Make You Rich!

"Jesus was rich, for YOUR sake He became poor, that through His poverty YOU might become RICH" (2 Cor.8:9)!

The verse is staggering in its implication. Traditional Christianity and Hellenistic mind-sets view this Scripture as a mystical or spiritual application – but it *really* is about our financial lives.

We are promised a heaven filled with streets of gold and pearly gates. But, are God's richness just for when you get to heaven? Sure, heaven is a place of abundance! But, this Scripture is NOT just talking about later - it is talking about having abundance in our NOW... *in this lifetime!*

The apostle that Jesus loved said, "*I pray that you prosper as your soul prospers*" (3 Jn. 1:2). Some people refuse to think that John was talking about the riches of finances, but if you are to prosper in EVERY area of your life... IT *MUST* INCLUDE YOUR FINANCES!

The greatest spiritual warfare in your life is to really believe what the Bible says about WHO you are in God and what belongs to you. The most violent warfare is in YOUR mind!!!

Victory comes as you accurately apply the power and authority of God's promises to your life! Prosperity is in the NOW! You already have total authority and you can live in life's fullness...

"God takes great pleasure in your PROSPERITY" (Ps.35:27)!

"Success is nothing more than a few simple disciplines, practiced every day; while failure is simply a few errors in judgment, repeated every day. It is the accumulative weight of our disciplines and our judgments that leads us to either fortune or failure." Jim Rohn

Biblical Prosperity is about the achievement and the ability to change your future and the future of your environment.

You Must Have A Conscious Awareness Of Being Abundant

Your life will conform to what you expect, declare, and do. It's about persistent faith and unrelenting focus. Jesus taught us that to him who is conscious of much, more will be given! (Lk. 12:48).

Get this -- God knows NO lack! Every promise He extends to us is to bless us and cause us to flourish. He wants His people to live in fertile land with endless opportunities to prosper (Micah 7).

ABUNDANT THINKING causes things to manifest in your life. It may seem like nothing is happening - but something is *always* happening when you believe.

- Think about when you win, not when you fail.
- Think about what makes you happy, not sad.
- Think about what you gain, not lose (the water glass being half full, not half empty).
- Think about what you have rather than what you don't have.
- Think about what works in your life right now.
- Think about doing what will bring you fulfillment.

Abundant thinking won't give up! Perseverance is required. Don't lose focus. Don't undo the process! Don't stop - even if it looks like the opposite is happening. Keep rising up!

You really need to believe that God's Word works to bring forth extreme abundance and prosperity to YOU (Jn. 10:10).

You can become effective and make a difference HERE on this earth.

The Power to Get Wealth

"The Lord gives YOU the POWER to get wealth" (Deut. 8:18; 1 Cron. 29:12)! That doesn't mean that God just rains down wealth from the sky like a gigantic slot machine. But God gives us strategy and POWER to get wealth.

This promise is a reconfirmation to what was promised Abraham (over four hundred years later). We are the seed of Abraham, and heirs to the provisions of his covenant with God. One of these great provisions is the phenomenal POWER to obtain wealth.

Notice also that the promise of the power to get wealth isn't bound by time. It is a forever promise! We see it valid four hundred years after it was given - and four thousand years makes no difference.

Wealth is GENERATED by those who have the power to make wealth. that means you don't sit around and expect God to directly give you money. Most of the time, He will give you the POWER to create wealth for yourself. It's called INTENTIONAL WEALTH!

WHY does God give you the power to get wealth? The answer comes right away in this Scripture! Wealth establishes the COVENANT of God. God's covenant is what we are talking about throughout this book! When you know who you are, you can begin to enact God's covenant.

"Wealth is the Power To Influence" Ap. John Kelly

Each believer should develop what is called "Redemptive Consciousness." It is the correct Kingdom transformational thinking that grows and expands. As believers, because of the work of the Cross and the indwelling Spirit of God, you gain the potential to influence the world for good.

You are blessed to be a blessing, to enjoy life and ALSO feed the hungry, clothe the naked, heal the sick, visit the prisoners, be hospitable to strangers and aliens (Mat.25:14-46), and to serve humanity. Abundance is about compassionately loving and serving the world.

"Those who try to do something and fail are infinitely better than those who try to do nothing and succeed." Lloyd Jones

Every day say, "My life is worth living well."

What are you grateful for?

CONFESSION: "Today I will disassociate myself from all strongholds that are resistant to change. I will do what I can to expose the death that is religion" (Lk. 13:3 MSG).

I am released from bad memories of the past. I purposefully focus my mind on God and His glorious prosperity promises.

Day 15 - Focus on Winning!

"Though no one can go back and make a brand new start, anyone can start from now and make a brand new ending." Carl Bard

Are you a victim or the Victor? Is this a time of pity or a time of expectation?

Do circumstances get you down? Why?

Victims

Your future is predetermined by your thoughts in this moment. So, if you want to change your future, you must change what you are thinking about right now.

Success is determined by your belief system and your thought patterns. If you act like a victim, guess what? That's the way you will be treated. And... you will be a victim!

Victims allow someone else to be in control of their choices.

Victims REACT because they don't know they have a choice. Living reactively drains energy and causes uncontrolled stress.

Victims collect information but never fully act on what they know to DO.

Those who play the game of life TO WIN take action on what they KNOW. Victors live decisively with a positive and thankful attitude that causes a spiritual force that resolves problems. Winners always ask, "What is my next choice!" If you show up to win, then you will end up winning.

A winning outlook profoundly effects your personality. The way your family, friends, yourself, and even how the world responds to you is determined by your attitude.

You can't change what you're willing to tolerate.

The Israelite spies could only see the opposition (giants in the land). Joshua and Caleb had a different attitude! They saw huge grapes not giants. They took victory. Caleb said, "I am well able to take this mountain!"

The Lord told Joshua "Keep therefore the words of this covenant and do them, that you may PROSPER in all that you do." Joshua had to continually meditate on the covenantal Word. ""Meditate (think about it over and over until your mind is saturated) and observe TO DO the word" (see Josh. 1:8).

Don't let the words of God depart from your eyes -and keep them inside your heart (your soul, mind, and emotions (Prov. 4:21).

Your conscious pursuit and your subconscious thought must be in agreement. If your awareness seeks one thing and your subconscious is not in agreement (wants something else), it is impossible to win.

Successful people absolutely and deeply believe that they have the ability to succeed and that they will succeed. They do not consider any other option. They think positively and act in accordance with their belief structure.

When problems come, do you "feel" energized and excited to overcome?

Finish this statement, "I'll not settle for less than _____

PROACTIVE: Victorious people know the most important rules of gaining prosperity and success in life is that you must *learn to act without reacting.* Or, you could say, learn to have a proactive approach and stop reacting. This is called disciplined thinking. It means you gain an objective perspective to see the reality of a situation and the ability to maintain a proper mental approach.

You don't really have any control over a lot of what happens - but you can control your victorious response to every situation. Look for ways to effectively manage every experience, whether it be an emergency, adversity, or difficulty.

Today's reality is the result of yesterday's choices!

Don't just allow life to happen and then respond to your circumstances. Make choices based on your values, standards, and goals. Your choices are what create your outcome.

When a person discovers his purpose, he stands at the gateway of winning.

Your success is powered by what is important to you. Learn to see beyond the present difficulty. Develop a mental guard over extreme reactions and emotions.

Create your life by consciously choosing to live by DESIGN rather than by default. Build up a strong desire to take responsibility for your destiny.

Write your confession here about being deliberate and proactive.

"Circumstance does not make the man, it reveals him to himself." James Allen

CONFESSION: *Today, I cross over into the Promised Land that flows with milk and honey. There, the place of abundance waits for me!*

Work on DOING your list!

Every day say, *"My life is worth living well."*

40 Days
on
Prosperity

Section #4, "Your Energy"

Passion

Energy

Enthusiasm

Rest

Day 16 - Focus on Your Passion

"It is only the minority of people who seek self-improvement or personal growth. This is because whatever one's self-criticisms, one secretly really believes that one's way of being is okay and probably the only correct one. They are alright as they are, and all problems are caused by other people's selfishness, unfairness, and by the external world." Dr. David R. Hawkins

Prosperity means having the resources to do your job and to fulfill our purposes on earth! Passion is the force of success that propels you to accomplish what you were created to achieve. Your passion drives you to the mark of the high calling (***).

What are Your Greatest Desires?

Ask in faith, nothing wavering... Whatever things YOU DESIRE, when you pray, believe that you receive them, and you will have them (Mk. 11:24).

What is your greatest passion? (Create a mental picture of what you want to do.)

Where do you want to live?

How do you want to contribute to society, humankind, etc.

It's not about good luck! Life won't happen by accident. Trust your passion. Don't settle for less than fulfilling your purpose.

- The Holy Spirit will enable you to accomplish God's will. He will give you impartation to bring substance and manifestation.

- The more you move into the direction of your destiny, the more God will be able to trust you.

- Respect your desires and believe that dream-seed will produce in your life.

- Allow your desire to become your daily meditation (Eph. 5:14-18 AMP).

As you continue on your journey in this book, your vision will be enlarged, adjusted, and expanded.

"Any inconsistencies between your vision and your present situation, should show you that one OR THE OTHER HAS TO CHANGE!" T. Byler

Desire Grows

"Divine desire" is the clue for your destiny. Desire and passion are the energy that cause the seed to grow, causes your talents to increase, and makes things happen.

Divine desire does not come from you or your selfish ambition. Godly desire is only energized by God's intention for you to fulfill your purpose. Divine desire leads you to your individual purpose. The energy to grow and become productive and fruitful comes from God's purpose.

Right now, the Lord is trying to move your forward into His DESIRE for your life. He wants to express Himself in you.

God almost always leads you from within. God's direction speaks to your soul, to your feelings, to your human spirit, and to your thoughts. His communication is often an imparted yearning, longing, and passionate desiring. The Holy Spirit leads you by Divine desire.

That frequency of desire seeks ways of expression. These divine cravings seek an outlet. When you don't follow this prompting or longing, you experience internal conflict and emotional reactions. Unexpressed desires leads to dissatisfaction in life (make the heart sick, Prov. 13:12).

Many Christians are disillusioned because their desire seems suppressed. Interrupted destiny cause emotional disruption. Much of the frustration and discontent you feel about how things are going in your life is a "Divine dissatisfaction." Dissatisfaction means it's time to change!

Godly desire fulfilled expresses itself in a more abundant life. Having desire fulfilled is a tree of Life (Prov. 13:12).

> **"I hope that I may always desire more than I can accomplish." Michelangelo Buonarroti**

Through Christ, We should rule and reign as kings in this life!
Rom. 5:217

Often, people won't appreciate your efforts or passions. Recognize that they don't see it yet – and don't get pent-up over other people's reactions, or their broken promises. Remember - it's your attitude about your progress that affects everything. Whether others recognize what you offer isn't the issue. What's important is the growth process of doing what is supposed to be done.

- How can your life have more meaning?

- How can you progress to the next level?

- Who can you help?

Right now, take a fresh sheet of paper and write at the top "In relationship to my life's vision, today I want to *feel*...." Then, present this in prayer and determination and set your day for expectations. (It's not all about DOING. You'll be amazed at the results! When your mind (thoughts) and body (feelings) align to your spiritual vision, you become WHOLE!) Try this every day!

Make these CONFESSIONS part of your weekly action plan.

I will always be honest in all my business dealings.

I will always work with great dedication.

I will always enjoy my work and take time for family and fun.

I will always be a student learning more and becoming more effective.

I will always take initiative and manage my time.

I will always do things in an excellent manner.

I will always be optimistic and enthusiastic.

I will always help other people and share.

I will always strive to be healthy and active.

What are you grateful for?

Every day say, "*My life is worth living well.*"

Day 17 - Focus on the Energy of Prosperity!

Where do you spend your energy?

Do you spend your energy on an hopeful, positive, and optimistic opportunities? Your WHYs convince your subconscious mind to be in agreement with your target! That agreement gives you energy! You must realize that if you are not purposefully conscious and aware of how you spend your energy, it can easily dissipate into non-creative and non-beneficial ways.

What ZAPS your energy?

- Embracing worry and fear drains energy.

- Procrastination drains energy.

- Wasting time drains energy.

- Being victimized exhausts your energy.

- Having poverty minded people around you drains your energy.

- Being anxious about success drains your energy

- Living a sad and nonproductive life weakens your energy.

- Defending your excuses gives energy to your fears and emphasizes your problems.

The Bible tells us of a divine force of energy that is normally invisible but can be revealed to us in the perceived result of produced light.

Aristotle (four centuries before Christ) stated that energy is the force of *dunamis* "power, capacity, and faculty." Energy is realized as potential is pursued and accomplished.

New Testament authors considered energy to be what activates power (*dunamis*). There are numerous uses of *enéryeia* "(energy), operative or actualizing power," *enérgema* "effect(iveness), function," *eneryés* "energetic, effective," and *eneryeln* "energize, set in motion, actualize."

Speaking of the Body of Christ, 1 Corinthians 12:6 says, "And there are differences of energizations (energy), but God is the identical One Who energizes everything in all things." Continuing in verses 10-11, "To another [is given] the energizations of potential(ities) ... but one and the same Spirit energizes all of these, allotting to each individual according as He wills."

Faith (*pistis*) is an energizing formation caused by love (2 Cor. 1:6, Gal. 5:6).

"The Word (referring to *logos*) is a rational principle energizing in believers..." (1 Thes. 2:13).

"The prayer of a righteous person energizes (Jms. 5:16).

"For it is God [Who is] energizing in you all both to will and to energize for the sake of being pleased" (Philp. 2:13).

"Faith energizing through love..." (Gal. 5:6).

Grace is "bestowed according to the energy of the power (*dunamis*) [of God (Eph. 3:7).

The Body of Christ is held together according to energy evident in Christ's Life (Eph. 4:16).

"For it is God (Who is) energizing (salvation) in you all both to will and to energize for the sake of His good pleasure" (Phil. 4:3 13).

"I labor, striving according to His Energy [that is] energizing itself (in) a natural capacity in me..." (Col. I:29)

Are you willing to GAIN energy to win? Will you learn to focus your energy, your thoughts, your time, your creativity into your dream?

Accomplishing goals is energizing. Energy causes you to want to work faster.

As believers, the POWER and energy by which we do things comes only through the Holy Spirit! He alone is the energy (*dunamis*) by which we operate (see my book Connecting for lots more on the subject of energy).

It isn't until you DO something that you discover that the secret to prosperity and success is already resident inside of you.

In this glorious time of vigorous CHANGE, you should expect to excel with greater expanding blessings, success, happiness, and prosperity.

Prosperity allows you to have the feeling of being fulfilled by what you do. Prosperity means that you appreciate and enjoy your life, your spiritual relationships, your career, and your family. Prosperity means that you have the ability to influence your present generation.

The Finished Work means that God has already done all He;s going to do about your prosperity - now it is up to you to apprehend it, to believe, and to do!

Right now, you and I should be thinking about the expansion of our lives. Life in the Spirit is all about LIFE (not death). It's all about being excited. Don't look back at the past one more time! Look ahead with anticipation.

Get smarter about the USE of YOUR TIME. Get help. Improve your NOW. Move into a positive direction. Shift into overdrive. You can't change the past. The future is uncertain – but you can live, and move, and have your BEING in the NOW (***).

Knowing where you are going keeps you from wasting time and effort doing meaningless things. Think about how easy you breathe - how natural it is - without mindful effort. Now, imagine all the BLESSINGS of God just flowing into your being - right NOW, just as easy as breathing! Attract Godly blessings, prosperity, and success by noticing how it comes to you unconsciously.

The wealth of the wicked is laid up for you (Prov. 13:22). You are a magnet!

Take your human (soul realm) effort off your expectations and allow God to lead you. Allow yourself the ability to hope and believe with yielded trust. That means you STAND without flailing about trying to *make things happen*. Allow resources and people to flow through you for your use.

There's a huge difference between thinking that you are doing God's business and allowing God to actually work through you.

Start Each Day Fast!

Advice from a trapeze artist, *"You don't have a long time to leave where you are to get where you are going."*

How can you transition speedily? There's a momentum in responding to the Spirit as soon as you can. The sooner you move into that new priority positioning, the sooner prosperity will manifest in your life.

"Things may come to those who wait...but only the things left by those who hustle." - Abraham Lincoln

Once you locate your TRUE calling, become productive, and engage in energized momentum you will find results. Action brings change. Decisions respond to the quick strike. Work fast and do ten times more than you did yesterday. Change your behavior through productive speed.

Work out of passion and not out of urgency.

Do it faster! One of the main things you can start doing today and every day from now on is to gain energy and momentum. Blast through. Start each day with faster productivity. Be decisive, responsive, resourceful. Momentum causes harmonic responses that amplify your life!

Think bigger! Slow is usually more difficult than fast because momentum brings excitement and energy. Don't wait for people to acknowledge you. Be proactive. Initiate your own opportunities rather than being passive.

A huge secret of success is learning to stop doing what doesn't work! Learn to quit FAST! Edison quit ten thousand times before he found success.

Look for the methods that work. No stress, no more procrastination, and no more hesitation. Gain urgency in your work today!

Why are you grateful today?

Every day say, "*My life is worth living well.*"

CONFESSIONS: *God energizes me NOW with hope and anticipation. I live in the NOW of ABUNDANT prosperity.*

Day 18 - Focus on Enthusiastic Prosperity!

We fail because of false expectations. We fail because of negative thinking. We fail because others try to take away our hope. It's easy to become discouraged these days. We really need to FOCUS on becoming energized and enthused.

After all, this is your life... and you and I need to break away from all the old religious barriers that speak limitation and opposition.

Enthusiasm is the greatest success and prosperity tool of all time! You need to properly engage your brain (mind, heart) and demand right thinking and correct responses to get ENTHUSED.

> *"It's faith in something and enthusiasm for something that makes a life worth living."* Oliver Wendell Holmes

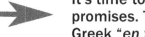 It's time to become enthused by God's ongoing promises. The word "enthusiasm" comes from the Greek "*en theos,*" which means becoming God-inspired. Imagine that! Enthused people embrace life with joy and exuberance. They know that God will INSPIRE them with the best in life.

The #1 definition in Webster's Dictionary for enthusiasm is: "*Belief in special revelations of the Holy Spirit.*" Notice, my friend, enthusiasm brings "special revelations!" Let this definition change your reality. Get your own "special revelation" about prosperity!

Special revelation will change your future. Your imagination will be inspired and guided in greater measure by the Holy Spirit. You must renew your MIND (Rom. 12) with the thoughts that will create a prosperous life. This continual process is known by scientists as imprinting or modeling. Whatever you call it, start now and just do it!

Influencing your mind to think upon certain spiritual truths can create a better future for you. Soooo.... please, get enthused about that!

It means that you decide WHAT needs to be changed in your outlook, your expectations, and your assumptions. Decide what will go into your personal mind/computer.

Enthusiasm is adventurous and dares to reach out past previous restrictions.

"Enthusiasm is one of the most powerful engines of success. When you do a thing, DO IT with your might. Put your whole soul into it. Stamp it with your own personality. Be active, be energetic, be enthusiastic and faithful, and you will accomplish your object. Nothing great was ever achieved without enthusiasm" - Ralph Waldo Emerson

Right now, take control of the caliber of information that you allow to enter into your subconscious mind.

Be positive and ENTHUSED about your future. Build new definitions of what you expect. Imagine positive and prosperous results.

What can you imagine that would enthuse you?

"Nothing great was ever achieved without enthusiasm."
Ralph Waldo Emerson

Most believers don't comprehend the Divine power and energy available for us to access success. The vitality of confidence. The momentum of accomplishing achievement reaches out and connects you to your destiny potential.

The Kingdom Reality of enthusiasm (*en-theos*, the special God inspired revelation that ignites you to be your best) is the forceful velocity of prosperity. There's a Divine symphonic resonance when we co-mingle in this sphere of enthusiastic dynamic power.

Enthusiasm is God's ENERGY.

Let's study this verse in 2 Corinthians 9:8-15, *"And God is able to make all grace abound toward you; that ye, always having all sufficiency in all things, may abound to every good work."*

First notice that "God is *able*." Surprisingly, *"able"* is the familiar Greek word *dunamis* that means power to reproduce itself, or dynamite, or ENERGY. This phrase is written in the Greek present tense and that means God's action "continues in this present time." He continuously brings forth creative energy NOW. God has the creative power to do it!

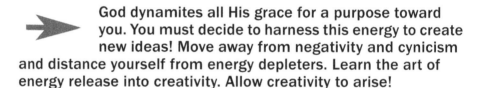

God dynamites all His grace for a purpose toward you. You must decide to harness this energy to create new ideas! Move away from negativity and cynicism and distance yourself from energy depleters. Learn the art of energy release into creativity. Allow creativity to arise!

In our Scripture above, look at the word *"abound,"* it means *"to have more than enough!"* Baur, Arndt and Gingrich (pg. 651) states that "abound" means, "to *be rich*, to *make extremely rich*". God power of GRACE causes you to "abound" so that extreme wealth can come your way.

- It's about having God's dynamite creative power in your life so that YOU can abound with energy and prosperity!

We can reword this Scripture to say, "And God, IS CONTINUOUSLY dynamiting all His creative grace to make you EXTREMELY RICH." WHY? So that you will have *"sufficiency in all things!"*

> This word *"sufficiency"* means: to ward off all hardship and lack - no matter what the circumstance. And, to allow yourself to creatively abound to every good work.

Next we find the word "abound" used twice in this Scripture. God's grace abounds in us so that His creativity brings extreme wealth and riches that will flood every good work! So... it's up to you to find out the unlimited good work the Lord wants you to abound toward.

True ENERGY is productive, automatic, and natural. It is not forced. Energy connects to and develops your talents and desires. Allow your dreams to empower your inventiveness.

"And God is able to make all grace abound toward you; that ye, always having all sufficiency (abundance, no lack) in all things, may abound to every good work" (2 Cor. 9:8-9).

"All the breaks you need in life wait within your imagination. Imagination is the workshop of your mind, capable of turning mind energy into accomplishment and SUCCESS." Napoleon Hill

RESULTS require *ACTION!* Don't hesitate to imagine and develop new ideas. You may feel that your missed your timing... or waited too long. But it's time to begin again with immediate actions. Action reinforces your faith that what you expect already exists. Reinforced ideas accelerate your creative energy.

Accelerate your creative energy to believe for what is already yours!

What can you do to have more energy?

What are you grateful for?

Be enthusiastic about DOING your list!

Every day say, "My life is worth living well."

CONFESSION: *I expect to receive! I expect success! I expect blessings... When I allow God's purposes to happen, soon great things will come to pass!*

Day 19 - Focus on Enthusiasm! #2

Passion and enthusiasm are such important topics, we need to set aside several days about it!

"All achievements, whether in the business, intellectual, or spiritual world, are the result of definitely directed thought, are governed by the same law and are of the same method. Whatever your present environment may be, you will fall, remain, or rise with your thoughts, your Vision, your Ideal. You will become as small as your controlling desire; as great as your dominant aspiration." Og Mandino

"Success is going from one failure to the next without a lessening of enthusiasm." Winston Churchill

Once you become **ENTHUSED** with expectation, everything changes. Your invigorated countenance becomes contagious. You sense new inspiration and motivation. New insights and ideas drop into your mind. You suddenly have greater focus, direction, intuition, and charisma.

Passion, confidence, fervor, and energy attracts people and causes incredible opportunities to come to you. That's the way it works. Those who have, get. Enthusiasm makes you a God inspired "success magnet."

"Every production of genius must be the production of enthusiasm." Benjamin Disraeli, (British Prime Minister & Novelist. 1804-1881)

What you are enthused about can only expand. Enthusiasm ignites your imagination. Enthusiasm builds your faith. It grows expectation.

Just imagine that your soul realm prospers! Isn't it exciting to think about enthusiasm and not about being depressed? Not being sad all the time? Your mind is a factory that creates Godly response upon this earth. Pray, "Thy Kingdom come - Thy will be done, on earth as it is in heaven." You are the earth – Right now - Right here!

"If you have zest and enthusiasm you attract zest and enthusiasm. Life gives back in kind." Norman Vincent Peal

Well, get excited and act like it has already happened! Think about how success will smell, feel, and taste.

- Enthusiasm is the energy produced as a result of positive expectation. It's just that easy.

- The more you think eagerly, ardently, expectantly, enthusiastically about your vision – the greater your results.

- Enthusiasm bonds you to a greater power of the Lord. You become deeply centered in the certainty that Biblical principles have a reality to you.

Biblical Mindsets

Scriptures about enthusiasm:

"He (Apollos) had been taught the way of the Lord and talked to others with great enthusiasm and accuracy..." (Acts 18:25).

"Since you excel in so many ways—you have so much faith, such gifted speakers, such knowledge, such enthusiasm, and such love for us—now I want you to excel also in this gracious ministry of giving" (2 Cor.8:7).
"I am thankful to God that he has given Titus the same enthusiasm for you that I have." (2 Cor. 8:16).

"For I know how eager you are to help, and I have been boasting to our friends in Macedonia that you Christians in Greece were ready to send an offering a year ago. In fact, it was your enthusiasm that stirred up many of them to begin helping" (2 Cor. 9:2).

"Work with enthusiasm, as though you were working for the Lord rather than for people" (Eph. 6:7).

Enthusiasm is living in the power of the Holy Spirit! It is co-existing on earth with heavenly presence. This is the hour to experience the supernatural in your life. Get rid of every glimpse of scepticism and intellectualism, and lean into supernatural expectations.

Ask, Seek, Knock

"Ask and it will be given to you. Search, and you will find. Knock, and the door will be opened for you." (Mat. 7:7)

We've been told this Scripture is about knocking continually or seeking continuously. However, The aorist imperative of these three verbs are COMMANDS.

- "ASK." Ask enthusiastically and in full confident faith expecting an answer!

- "KNOCK." enthuSiastically knock on the door of opportunity and find it is already open."

- "SEEK." You enthusiastically seek and expect answers to manifest your purposes into this world.

CONFESSION: *The only thing I can change is me - and when I change, my future changes! I ask for productivity. I seek for wholeness. I knock on the door of my heart and find it open. I take the risk to believe and become extremely successful! I no longer worry about occasional failures... I take the offensive - and refuse defensive posture or passive outlooks. I embrace change - knowing that nothing changes until I do!*

Day 20 - Focus on Rest

Let out a little more string on your kite. – Alan Cohen

After you gain true enthusiasm, you can begin to understand rest. Rest is not passive or inactive, but it is peaceful and filled with positive anticipation (like waiting for a baby to be born).

On the 7th day of creation, God "rested" (Gen. 2:1-3). That doesn't mean He's asleep! This Hebrew word translated here as "rested" is the verb *shabath*, which is translated in English as "SABBATH."

Interestingly, the primary meaning of this word is not "rest," in terms of relaxing or rejuvenating,

The day of rest was different than the other days of creation. It belongs to Him; Jesus is Lord of the Sabbath (MK 2:28). It is His.

God *blessed* the Sabbath day of rest (Ex. 20:8-11). Earlier we talked about how the word "BLESS" means to give favor, to endue with power for success, prosperity, fecundity, longevity, etc." REST is how you enter into this time of BLESSING.

Many years ago, when earnestly praying for a greater move of the Holy Spirit, the Lord spoke to me saying, "The servant of the Lord must not strive" (2 Tim. 2:24). That was a pivotal moment in my life - realizing that God already WANTS to bless us – and our travail won't make something happen. Striving opposes blessing.

- This is the 7th thousandth year from the Fall - or the 7th Day of rest. We live in the perpetual Sabbath.

- For Christians, every day becomes our Sabbath - and we enter into His blessed rest every day. Each day is a time to be endued with power for success and prosperity!

The Spies

The spies went into the Promise Land for 40 days. Because of their failed perceptions (seeing the enemy like giants and themselves as grasshoppers), God told them they had to wander in the wilderness for forty years (a year for each day of unbelief and striving). Hebrews tells us it was because of their unbelief that they could not enter into the rest of the Promised Land (Heb. 4:3, 5). Not having rest was described as "unbelief."

God said to them, "You will know My rejection" (Num. 14:34). Wow! Strong words because they were in unbelief and couldn't find rest! How about you? Do you see yourself as incapable of defeating the giants in your land? Do you feel like you are endlessly wandering in the wilderness? Are you going around the same ol' mountain over and over again?

Do You Try to Do Too Much!?

The number one barrier to finding rest is hyper-busyness. Just because you are super busy does not mean you are making progress or gaining success.

It's only too easy to feel exhausted from trying to do too much. If you're feeling worn out, discouraged, or overwhelmed, it ONLY can mean that you're making things too hard. This over-burdening actually resists your own success.

The "information age" has just "too much" information. It's easy to become bombarded with all kinds of stuff you don't really need. Be aware of what is necessary to learn that will make a long term difference in your life. Know your limits. Be selective about which information you will learn. Trust your intuition.

 Most people miss 90% of their life because of doing busy work. God is not a cruel taskmaster Who wants to exhaust you. Nor will He require you to build the kingdom by works. God wants relationship and He wants you to enjoy the life you have. He gives you a glorious gift of time. A gift of beauty. A joy to be fulfilled. As you plan for your future, plan for no more striving.

You don't have to win the whole world.

Moses was told a great a truth, "Moses, you are doing too much! Start working smarter by training others to do what you are doing. Don't burn out!" (See Exodus 18:13-27.) Moses changed two things that positively transformed his life and ministry:

> His way of thinking,

> His way of working.

Lesson learned:

- The less you do, the more you accomplish.

- The more you delegate, the better it works!

- The more you facilitate others to accomplish, the less you need to do.[1]

- God does not get tired (Is. 40:28)!

 Busy minds must learn to value the present moment. That means when you're at work, you're not worrying about home and vice-versa. In order to do that, all unfinished work and responsibilities must be captured in some way. Always take a tablet with you. Write your "to do next" down so you don't try to carry all that information in your mind. Make lists of what needs to be accomplished next! Always ask, "What's next!"

This step will help you relieve pressure and undo stress. Clearly make written distinctions about all of your commitments. Write them down - and you won't be so distracted.

You can project the value of having peace every moment of every day.

- That means you'll have to guard against combustible relationships that drag you down.

---

1.   Keith Johnson, The Confidence Coach Blog, Feb. 2010

- You need to learn to schedule your life with ample time to rest.

- Peace is more than calmness - or coping with your surroundings. It's more than mere survival – it's becoming what *shalom* means, being WHOLE.

Success always harmonizes with peace as creating the best principles of living.

Peace is always present once you stop disrupting it!
Peace is only a thought away.

Regardless how well you master the art of schedules and plans, you can't control all external circumstances. Sorry...

Ask yourself:

- Have I entered into rest?

- Do I completely trust God? Or do I murmur and complain?

- Do I know where I'm going? Do I know who I am in God?

- Do I wait for things to happen or do I cause them to happen?

- Do I study the Word of God and believe what it says over my life?

Don't try to "Make it happen" – but "Let it" happen!

Rest is not apathy and doing nothing. Rest moves assuredly and peacefully in the right direction.

Rest is ACTION without a sense of "having" to do something. The closer you get, the more excited you will become – which brings you even closer! Your works are a demonstration of your faith! (Jam. 2:17). Keep sensitive to the voice of the Lord.

Rest is an energy of passionate intent and not obligation or duty.

Rest is not about controlling everything in life. It's about flowing with it.

"Submit to God and be at peace with him; in this way, prosperity will come to you" **(Job 22:21).**

Make a list of what can you stop doing that isn't necessary to your dreams?

Learn to say "NO."

The only reason you don't receive what the Bible promises is because you hold on to some form of resistance to rest. You're NOT stuck, you know. You can get rid of old baggage.

Take a look at what is not working in your life. What can you let go? If you decide to let go of something, you don't have to figure out a complex way to do it - expect change to be easy. New ideas will come to you. A sense of relief comes when you get on track!

Success is not just about working harder. Trying too hard can cause frustration and restrict your imagination. Being too attached to the outcome of a project can cause obsessive behaviors. Put yourself into trust and rest. If God said it, He will do it! Let the peace of God connect you to the finished work!

Principles To Never Forget.

- Stress is a distortion of what God intends for your life.

- Peace is ever present.

- Confusion keeps us from finding peace.

- Abundance is a current reality, poverty is an alteration.

CONFESSION:
Dis-stress has no place in me! Peace fills me with direction and purpose. It is morning and joy has come! I am energetic and ready to GO!

40 Days
on
Prosperity

Section #5, "Your Values"

Values

Courage

Confidence

Excellence

Creativity

Day 21 - Focus on Your Core Values!

"Try not to become a man of success but rather to become a man of value." Albert Einstein

Before you can actualize Godly prosperity, you must determine your core values. Values are the non-negotiable and never changeable considerations of your life. They are the pivotal absolutes and inner beliefs that you cherish and they are the principle cores that govern everything in your life. They are what you will pay a price to maintain.

When you establish your values, you must come into full agreement with them and act with unswerving authority to enforce them in your life.

Values are essential to effective leadership and prosperity. They are the uncompromisable, undebatable certainties that compel your behavior. Values give you motivation and they are the reason *why* you make choices to do things. Values determine your boundaries concerning your conduct. Values that provide certain direction in spite of your emotions.

Values transcend self-centeredness. Values could be things like honesty, integrity, morality, peace and tranquility, beauty, and family. All the things that you value must also be considered as you target your life. Focus on what you are doing right in your life.

All improvement in your life begins when you clarify your true values and then commit to live by them.

What do you believe in and stand for and how will that translate into your prosperity?

> *BLESSED (Happy, fortunate, prosperous, and enviable) is the person... who's delight and desire are in the law of the Lord, and on His law (the precepts, the instructions, the teachings of God) he habitually meditates (ponders and studies) by day and by night. And he shall be like a tree firmly planted [and tended] by the streams of water, ready to bring forth its fruit in its season;... and everything he does shall PROSPER [and come to maturity].*
> Ps. 1:1-3 Amp.

We can't make up our own rules and expect God to bless them. We need to incorporate His values into our lives. Determining your list of core values will be one of the most important keys to your success. You should carry this with you and embed your values upon your mind and heart.

Write what it means to you to live a Biblical life of value.

Every aspect of your life should define and be defined by your values. Successful people prosper because they are very clear and concise about their values. Unsuccessful people are usually uncertain or do not have values.

> *"Happiness is that state of consciousness which proceeds from the achievement of one's values."*–Ayn Rand

When choice comes, VALUES determine what to do next. They create absolute freedom, contentment, and stability. Values allow you to enjoy the process of fulfilling what you desire and deserve. Real life comes from defining and following your value system. Every situation and every experience must serve this purpose of Godly love.

Your life must become VALUE and character driven and NOT personality driven.

David asked about several values in Psalm 15: *"Lord, who may dwell in your sanctuary? Who may live on your holy hill? He whose walk is blameless and who does what is righteous, who speaks the truth from his heart and has no slander on his tongue, who does his neighbor no wrong and casts no slur on his fellowman, who despises a vile man but honors those who fear the Lord, who keeps his oath even when it hurts, who lends his money without usury and does not accept a bribe against the innocent. He who does these things will never be shaken."*

- Notice it is the one who "speaks the truth from his heart" (v. 1-2).

- He values kindness, he "does his neighbor no wrong" (v. 3).

- He values his word, he "keeps his oath even when it hurts" (v. 4).

- He values justice because he "does not accept a bribe against the innocent" (v. 5).

What other values do you find in this verse above?

Maintaining values (standards) brings confidence and emotional and spiritual stability. We can't be one way at work and another way at home. In order to prosper, we must completely integrate Godly values into *all* spheres of life.

We should be careful not to judge others and their choices of values. Just establish your own.

Seriously consider what new values you need to incorporate in your life.

> **Prosperity consciousness is being aware of your VALUES!**

Consider as values: spirituality, honesty, wisdom, virtue, ethics, courage, persistence, humor, generosity, integrity, kindness, modesty, prudence, creativity, comfort, acceptance, commitment, sacrifice, vitality, intelligence, fairness, justice, mercy, humility, appreciation of all things, hope, curiosity, learning, gratitude, understanding, and accountability. Don't forget compassion, hard work, and diligence.

Go back to your list of 8 important things you want to accomplish soon, and make sure they fit into your value system. Do they need adjustments?

Solomon's Success & Value Secrets:

More than three thousand years ago, King Solomon said, "Money answers all things!" (Ecc. 10:19) Today we say, "Money talks!"

As we have studied, we see that the Bible doesn't oppose money - money is not the root of all evil. But, Solomon had lots of money, and he couldn't find peace.

Money can buy choices!

Money can't buy you real friends or forgiveness. But, money can answer the situations for which it was designed. It can buy the opportunity to have choices.

King Solomon had a lot to say about prosperity depending upon your diligence and pursuit of excellence. *"Fools fold their hands and consume their own flesh* and can even kill them" (Prov. 21:25). He tells you to not just sit around talking about doing something (Prov.14:23).

Solomon spoke of establishing the right business even before domestic comfort 1) *Prepare your outside work, 2) make it fit for yourself in the field; 3) and afterward build your house (Prov. 24:27).* Solomon insists that work provides the engine for prosperity.

1. Get professional advice from the best sources (Prov.15:22, 20:18).

2. Plan your work and work your plan. (Prov. 21:5).

3. Follow the procedures no matter what (Ecc 8:6).

4. Don't chase silly ideas– work industriously (Proverbs 12:11, 28:19).

5. Don't get involved with "get rich quick" schemes - but use conscientious preparation (Prov.1:30-33).

6. Stop sleeping all the time and.... work (Prov. 6:6-11).

7. Don't borrow - produce (Prov. 22:7).

8. Don't spend all your money on lavishness – save for your future (Prov. 21:17).

9. Don't daydream of upcoming opportunities – work on the here and now. (Prov. 17:24).

10. Expand your enterprises (Ecc 11:2).

11. Work progressively and consistently - without haste (Prov. 19:2, 21:5).

Work on DOING your list!

Memorize this verse: "I am the Lord your God, Who teaches you to profit" Isaiah 48:17

Every day say, "My life is worth living well."

CONFESSION: *God has incredible things in store for me today!*

Day 22 - Focus on Courage

"Courage is resistance to fear, mastery of fear -- not absence of fear. It is acting in spite of it." Mark Twain

The opposite actions to counter against poverty, rejection, fear, and discouragement are COURAGE and BOLDNESS. The more difficulties you overcome, the more courageous you become. Courage matters today and every day.

- Courage thrives under pressure and difficulty. It is aggressive and creative.

- Courage grows in strength when opposed.

- Courage proclaims your present dreams because you deserve to be heard.

- Courage is the foundation of strong character.

- Courage gives you the ability to move forward in Faith - no matter what!

"Be of good COURAGE, and he shall strengthen your heart..." (Ps. 31:24).

In the Chinese language, the words *crisis* and *opportunity* are the same word. That's a good way to look at your life today. Viewing current problems as opportunities causes a improved sense of purpose and boldness about everything in your life.

Problems must be faced and solved. Solving problems makes people prosper!

When it seems that all is lost, don't give up! Constant obstacles don't mean you should quit - they can be evidence of progress.

"You gain strength, courage and confidence by every experience in which you must stop and look fear in the face. You must do the thing you think you cannot do." Eleanor Roosevelt

> "In life, you are rewarded in direct proportion to the problems you solve."
> Mark Gorman

Don't rely on others to empower you or to encourage you. You need to face your assignments and destiny with assertive and aggressive bravery.

The greatest key to getting rid of fear and finding courage is to think BIG. You can achieve - you can win. Courage allows all that is rightfully yours come to you. If you don't indisputably believe, with everything that is in you, that prosperity is yours and that the goals that you are asking for are attainable, then you aren't thinking courageously.

Courage is Indispensable- characteristic of prosperous living - you must have it!

 Courage causes you to attempt the adventurous and impossible. You can make history if you press the limits. You're the one to make things happen! Practice daring boldness and audacity in all things:

- Courage accelerates your success.

- It brings targeted tactical application.

- It builds your confidence and boosts you through the hindrances of life.

- Courage takes risks. It propels, motivates, energizes and empowers.

- Courage demands an aggressive and strategic attack against all that hinders.

- Courage brings energy.

- Courage can be observed through your words and actions.

- Courage builds the WILLPOWER to follow through.

- True courage propels you to move away from the mundane and familiar and enter the unknown.
- Courage and bravery leads, motivates, and inspires.

You can't be brave if you've only had wonderful things happen to you. –Mary Tyler Moore

Courage and boldness help remove uncertainties, apprehensions, and doubts related to prosperity lurking in your subconscious mind.

"Courage is rightly considered the foremost of the virtues because upon it, all others depend." Winston Churchill

"What would life be if we had no courage to attempt anything?" Vincent Van Gogh

How will you act with courage today? (What do you plan today?)

Biblical Mindset

JEHOVAH CHAYEL (*chayil*): There is power in this Name of God. The Hebrew word *Chayel* appears over 230 times and is a symbol and a word often translated 'living.'

Chayel also means a courageous army, wealth obtained through military strength, bravery, virtue, valiant, valor, strength, able, a great company, might, power, riches, great substance. The Chayel was worn as a medallion around the neck along with the Star of David. It can be translated:

* The Lord God is my Life
* The Lord God is my Strength
* The Lord God is my wealth and my power
* The Lord God is my army
* My Great riches are of the Lord God.

Jehovah Chayel enables you to advance to a higher level of strength, wealth, and valor that will cause you to stand before open doors of opportunities even with kings and dignitaries.

Every day say, *"My life is worth living well."*

Day 23 - Focus on Confidence!

Statistics tell us that 85% of the population has low self esteem and lack of confidence. In fact, It is the #1 reason why many people fail to accomplish their dreams. A lack of confidence will also be obvious in all that you do.

My friend, IF you underestimate your self-worth, or you allow someone else's opinion of you to hinder you, then you will stay deprived, anesthetized, and underprivileged.

A lack of confidence can affect every area in your life. Low self-esteem is usually manifested along with things like:

- Being frustrated or angry
- Feeling unloved or unlovable
- Feeling worried, insecure, and/or shy
- Fear of failure
- Fear of really being yourself
- Procrastination and having unmet expectations
- Feeling unfulfilled
- Being indecisive
- Feeling unimportant and without abundance, significant relationships, happiness, or satisfaction

The definition of confidence is, "the state or expectation of being certain." The definition of "expectation" is "anticipating with confidence and certainly that you will have what you want (fulfillment).

Confidence is not about what happens "around" you, it is what is deeply rooted inside you. Confidence is about BEING. It is the expression of Who God is in you. Who you are inside creates the outcome of everything that happens. Change yourself on the inside and change your results.

FAITH is the expression of confidence and certainty in God's Word that allows you to live it out (paraphrase Heb. 11:1).

1. Confidence is freedom from doubt. It is belief in yourself and your God-given abilities. (syn: assurance, self-assurance, self-confidence, authority, sureness).

2. Confidence is a feeling of trust (in someone or something); "I have confidence in you."

3. A state of confident hopefulness causes FAVOR in your life.

4. Confidence in your identity and your purpose builds unmovable self-esteem and personal character.

Self confidence allows you to commit to living a life consistent with your dreams. Self confidence gives greater competency in the accomplishing the goals you already set for yourself. Right choices bring a surge of mental energy. You become WHOLE and centered.

Confidence draws abundant LIFE into your reality. You will find that Divine favor rests upon you. Confidence causes the resources that you need to become evident. Confidence means you have learned to love yourself!

"The goal of every Christian is to learn how to THINK new! If we will think on God's level, we will live on His level."
Dr. LaDonna Osborn

"To love oneself is the beginning of a lifelong romance."
Oscar Wilde

Biblical Mind-sets About Confidence

You will become what YOU believe yourself to be.

We remember how Joshua and Caleb saw the giants in the land as grasshoppers - while the rest of the spies were defeated because what they saw produced fear.

You must recondition your mind to believe that you are handpicked to live confidently in this day! When you are convinced of who you are IN CHRIST, then what was once perceived as an obstacle, now become the sturdy but flexible pole necessary to vault over every hurdle.

You will become what you believe yourself to be.

Write out why YOU can be confident? 2 Cor. 3:5:

"The LORD is my light and my salvation; whom shall I fear? the LORD is the strength of my life; of whom shall I be afraid? Though an host should encamp against me, my heart shall not fear: though war should rise against me, in this will I be CONFIDENT."
(Ps. 27:1-3)

"Cast not away your CONFIDENCE... that after you have done the will of God, you can receive the promise." (Heb. 10:35-36)

MEMORIZE this verse TODAY:

"And THIS IS THE CONFIDENCE THAT WE HAVE IN HIM, that, if we ask any thing according to his will, He hears us: And if we know that He hear us, whatsoever we ask, we KNOW that we have the petitions that we desired of Him" (I Jn. 5:14-15)

If you were to act more confidently, how would that be?

ASSIGNMENT: Create a picture board of the life you want to live. Continue to have a positive inner attitude and you will change your reality.

You will know if your attitude has changed because it will be reflected (mirrored) back to you by those around you. When you are positive, optimistic, and self confident, then people will respond to you that way. Guard your thoughts and emotions carefully.

Be certain that you BE who you want to become.

Confidence comes with practice. Practice makes perfect. IF you know you're doing the right thing, then keep on doing it. That's where you get self confidence!

Michael Jordan discussed how he gained confidence, "*If I stood at the free throw line and thought about the 10 million people watching on the other sided of the camera lens, I couldn't have made any shots. I mentally tried to put myself in a familiar place. I think of all those time I shot free-throws using the same motion and same technique I've used thousands of times. You forget about the outcome. You know you're doing the right thing. So you relax and perform. After that you can't control anything anyway. It's out of your hands. You just don't worry about it.*"

Gaining confidence must not be a hobby! Activate the Kingdom dynamics of ruling and reigning with God! Start today.

All of God's resources and creative abilities are available to YOU!

CONFESSIONS: (Say out loud)

I am empowered to prosper and be a blessing! I am a confident overcomer and champion. My emotions are healthy. I have a prosperous mental and spiritual attitude.

No weapon or person can prosper against me. I live in joy, peace, and supernatural abundance. God has already given me the ability to deliver and perform in a given situation. I can do what no one has done yet, go where no one has gone yet.

I can BE who I've never been yet. Comprehend what I've never known before. I can do what nobody else thinks I can do. There are many things that I excel at. Suddenly, I can understand what I could not understand before. I can finish what I plan to do.

I will accomplish my full potential and destiny, I am satisfied, content, and relaxed as I progressively move forward to greater vision. I love the challenge of overcoming every obstacle. I climb several levels higher. Go BIG. Live to win! Go. Go. Go. Every single day I am convinced that I have what it takes.

Add some courageous ideas to the same 8 goals you've been working on.

1.
2.
3.
4.
5.
6.
7.
8.

You can build self confidence by simply taking small continuous steps forward toward your goals.

Every day say, "My life is worth living well."

 GET RID OF IT! One of the main strategies to create confidence and prosperity is to get rid of what you don't need. When you get rid of the unwanted, it causes a vacuum that draws your desires into place!

Maybe, you're like a lot of people... and have lots of clutter and things you don't use. Can you jam anything else in your closet? Or, do the clothes you have make you feel confident and self assured? Having too much excess causes negative feelings.

If you're hoarding in fear of loss in difficult times, you shut off the joy of freedom and expansion. It's time to clear out old toys, furniture, paper, magazines, and make room for the next level in your life. Get organized and gain control. Throw away and give away to increase your abundance.

How can you know what you really need until you get rid of what isn't working? New opportunities need uncluttered spaces! Go do this today!

Day 24 - Focus on Excellence!

Obtaining prosperity is not about anybody else but you.

Your willpower cannot persuade God to make you prosperous, nor can you force things to happen for you. You can't make people do what you want or need. You can't make the moon look bigger, or the fish swim your direction. The Book of Job reminds us that you can't make the sea leave it's banks.

The only good place to you use willpower is upon yourself in order to focus on positive predetermined vision. Diligently hold yourself accountable to respond correctly. Use willpower to guard your thoughts. To subdue doubt and negativity. And... you can use your willpower to increase your work with excellence.

> "You cannot teach a man anything; you can only help him find it within himself."
> Galelio

 Good things happen automatically as your desire for excellence draws God's power to yourself.

"A man is not rightly conditioned until he is a happy, healthy, and prosperous being; and happiness, health, and prosperity are the result of a harmonious adjustment of the inner with the outer of the man with his surroundings." – James Allen

Diligence

Diligence gets you there! On another sheet of paper write out: Psalm 119:4, 3-5, 7:15, 7:14-16. Proverbs 10:4, 10:3-5, 11:27,

11:26-28, whole 11th Chapter, 12:24, 12:23-25, 12:27. 26-28, 13:4-5, 21:4-6, 22:29, 22:28-29, 23:1-3, 27:22-24,

Excellence

Mediocrity is a choice; it's not always a conscious choice, but it is still a choice. Excellence never happens accidentally; it always happens because of purposeful decisions. Excellence is a habit to develop. You can begin today by deciding on ways to make quality choices. Never do mediocre work.

Excellence will challenge and consciously improve your inner thoughts, dreams, hopes, desires, values, and behaviors. It is about an obsessive desire to continually increase and move toward your purpose.

- Excellence activates awareness and enlarges your enjoyment of the present moment.

- Excellence causes you to stand out from others.

- Doing things well changes how you feel about yourself.

- It also importantly affects how others respond to you.

- Finding excellence is not about doing more things - just doing things better.

    ASK: *"Is what I'm doing right now truly reflective of a life committed to excellence?"* Gary Ryan Blair

> By mastering excellence in everything you do, you build a pathway to prosperity.

Excellence is not a one-time deal: it's an **ALL THE TIME DEAL!** Successful people realize that winning is always within their reach, and they have what it takes. Excellence is increased as you learn and improve each process.

You GENERATE prosperity rather than just hoping and waiting for it to happen to you.

Excellence is only attained by those who want to be the best! They plan to INTENTIONALLY succeed. Intentional excellence and maximum achievement means you've already won.

Reach out today to express the God inside of you. Think and act like God indwells you! Your uppermost purpose is to excellently express the maximized potential you have been given. Always stretch out to continue to improve all that you do.

EXCELLENCE is a purposeful and correct process of well done step by step accomplishments. When doing excellently, every decision, choice, and opportunity matters. Always commit to doing right.

 Excellence is the only standard by which you must live your life. To find True prosperity, everything accomplished must have excellence.

You don't need validation from others when you live your life by the standards of excellence.

What is your best course of action to increase excellence in your life?

In the list of 8 important things you want to accomplish next, write how each goal can be executed with excellence?

1.
2.
3.
4.
5.
6.
7.
8.

What are you grateful for today?   Work on DOING your to do list!

Every day say, "My life is worth living well."

Nothing is impossible for you if you believe!

Day 25 - Focus on Creativity!

"I saw the angel in the marble and carved until I set him free."
Michelangelo Buonarroti

Are you open to new creative ideas about becoming prosperous? Creative Ideas get you out of the BOX! Ghandi is famous for saying, *"Be the change that you want to see."*

Too Busy You can't be creative if you don't make time for it! If it is always about company, interruptions, and never a quiet moment - then there's no way for a creative idea to enter your mind!!!

"How many times does a brilliant idea pop into your head but you don't do anything about it? Ideas without execution amount to... well, diddly squat!" Success Magazine, Feb. 2010

Creativity can solve problems and bring answers to your life!

Creative people think about their dreams and keep their eyes open for new opportunities. They experiment and change the way they think. Creativity is the door to innovation and the portal to spontaneity. It is the expression of the Divine.

Do you ever just think about how creative the Holy Spirit is? Inside of you lives the answer to everything. Are you expecting a Divine idea? The Spirit of God has things to tell you. Don't be too busy to hear what He has to say. Meditate on the Word.

All the creativeness that you need for today is already inside you.

Creativity, revelatory ideas, and insight are expressions of the Divine. God gives incredible ideas that were not existent before.

Too Rigid   Being rigid in your mind-set won't allow you to live in this fast changing world. If you tenaciously hold on to all your favorite old ideas, you close up the lid to all new possibilities.

> *"The way to get good ideas is to get lots of ideas and throw the bad ones away."* Linus Paulding

To be creative, you must become less rigid and more curious about what is going on around you. Too many believers are closed to even the smallest deviation or "new idea." The more you are open to learn new technologies and new ideas, the less you feel cynical or anxious by inevitable change.

Creativity is the door to innovation and the portal to spontaneous "suddenlies!"

The rule of the Scriptures is creative abundance. Heaven is ever expanding goodness. Since you can be creative and change, take time to enter into that inner expansion.

- Look beyond the problems to imaginative solutions.

- Extend your imagination, but don't be ridiculous.

- Turn your circumstances into opportunities. The key is how you react to your situations. See a thousand opportunities!

- Look for and describe a need. Does it have value to others? Are they willing to pay for it?

- Trust your own personal creativity.

- Allow others to give you new ideas that you incorporate in your plan.

- Enjoy your Imagination as wonderful and not as a threat.

- Be alert to what new ideas have crossed your mind lately.

> *"Dream lofty dreams, and as you dream, so shall you become. Your vision is the promise of what you shall one day be; your ideal is the prophecy of what you shall at last unveil."*
> James Allen

Creativity means you are able to embrace change and enjoy what true success is all about!

What bothers you the most about this world where you live? (This is a key to creative prosperity.)

Can you look beyond the problems to imaginative solutions?

Are you intentionally moving forward to better yourself?

You must continuously be innovative and collaborative with the energy needed to accelerate into breakthrough ideas.

Your FOCUS on creativity will help establish the Kingdom of God in this earth! You are only one idea away from a miracle!

"There are no great people in this world, only great challenges which ordinary people rise to meet." William Frederick Halsey, Jr.

Every day say, *"My life is worth living well."*

Look again at the same list that you have been developing (8 important things) and search for a few new creative ideas that can make them more impactive.

Your creativity connects you to your destiny.

CONFESSION:

I love to create new ideas! I love the challenge of developing new concepts. I cherish the times of inspiration. The Lord continually downloads answers that I can understand and use. I am beyond excited to discover what will unfold next!

40 Days
on
Prosperity

Section #6, "Personal Decisions!"

Vision

Goals

Plans & Strategy

Priorities

Changing and Managing

Finishing Well

Day 26 - Focus on Your Prosperous Vision!

Today we begin to formulate and assemble your life's vision. This will grow and change as you progress through this book. You need to review your dream, your passion, and your talents. Engage with open-ended questions like: "What's my purpose on earth?" "What would it look like if it all worked out?"

 Ask yourself, "How can my life become a full investment into the cause for which Christ died? What does God require of me?" How can I cause every moment to be sensitive of the presence of God living in my NOW?

- A Godly vision will seem to be impossible. *Jesus said, "How MUCH MORE will your Father who is in heaven give good things?"* Matt. 7:11

- If you have a real vision, everything it takes to accomplish it will be worth it!

- A valid vision allows you to say, "I know where I'm going!"

- The provision for the vision Is In your house!

"The vision is not a castle in the air, but a vision of what God wants you to be. Let Him put you on His wheel and whirl you as He likes, and as sure as God is God and you are you, you will turn out exactly in accordance with the vision. Don't lose heart in the process. If you have ever had the vision of God, you may try as you like to be satisfied on a lower level, but God will never let you." Oswald Chambers

Many fail because they have unrealistic expectations. Let's face it, I'll never become a Dallas Cowboy cheerleader – no matter how much I set my mind to it, no matter how much I pray, no matter how much I confess and hope. I won't get any younger, and I won't suddenly become an athlete. Be expansive, but don't be ridiculous. If you're four feet tall, you'll probably never play in the NBA.

Up to now, you have been discerning between those presumptuous ideas and determining the real ones. You started with the most obvious needs, your dreams, values, passions – and now it's time to move forward and combine all this to gain greater effectiveness. Your LIFE VISION is the KEY that fulfills God's purpose for your life. The source of your vision comes from God's intention for your life.

Taking account of all that you have already accomplished during this study, we will continue to formulate your life's vision. Your talents and gifting cause you to have the potential to fulfill your vision.

The Lord asked Jeremiah, "What do you SEE?" And that is true with us! If we can SEE the possibility, then we can do it.

My favorite quote is by Helen Keller, *"The greatest tragedy in life is people who have sight but no vision."*

Forget about blurred wishes. Go beyond the expectation of others. A vision will specifically target your purpose.

If you want your vision to be made apparent, you need distinct, specific, and articulate statements. What will it look like? Exactly. What color? What style?

Have a clear and unwavering picture and FOCUS your heart upon that picture. Make ways for this desire to magnetically stay FIXED in your mind. Continuously meditate and build detail of what you want.

Biblical mind-set About Vision:

The VISION: Let's examine several translations of what Habakkuk said about the rampart. 2:1 *I will climb my watchtower* (station or better, "STAND myself on the RAMPART") *now and WAIT to* (look forth to) *SEE what answer* (what He will speak with me) *God will give to my COMPLAINT* (or what answer I am to give concerning this complaint) (NKJ, TLB, NIV, ASV combined).

The Rampart

The Hebrew word translated as *rampart* means encirclement; but the general sense of the word is that of the front line of defense that protected a city.[1] (Of course, we also see the typology that Jesus Christ is the High Tower that we can run into.)

A rampart is a watchtower, or battering ram tower consisting of an elevated and often portable structure that was positioned on top of a city wall. The watchman peered over the city wall and observed the attacking enemy. From this protected vantage point, he would then tell his soldiers how to gauge a counter attack.

Stand & Guard

Why did Habakkuk stand? He stood to keep watch and guard. In this case, he guarded standing like a watchman. This word "*standing*" is synonymous to the meaning we have discussed before when God put Adam into the Garden of Eden to "dress it and to <u>keep it</u>" (tend and guard, Gen. 2:15). Above all, you must tend and guard your vision.

We also see that standing/guarding is in Genesis 26:5, "Because that Abraham obeyed my voice, *AND KEPT MY CHARGE,* my commandments, my statutes, and my laws."

Proverbs uses this word of guarding "To watch" one's mouth (Prov. 13:3), the tongue (Ps. 34:13), and the lips (Ps. 141:3). It's our job to guard our garden vision.

Habakkuk STOOD on the rampart. Vines Expository Dictionary explains various ways of standing. One may "stand" for a definite purpose at a particular spot: "...stand upon the rampart..." From

---

1. From Nelson's Illustrated Bible Dictionary) (Copyright (C) 1986, Thomas Nelson Publishers)

the basic meaning of this verb comes the definition "to be established, immovable, and standing upright" on a single spot. The verb can suggest being "immovable," or "to abide and remain."

Wait

This word *wait* is also translated, "SET." Or, established so that the person will not fall over. Like the crouching catcher waiting to catch the baseball. Habakkuk waited and would not be moved.

- This waiting is expectant, strong, firm, and unmovable.

- Sometimes, waiting seems to take forever. It took Israel forty years to climb out of the desert, Jesus waited all his life until He was 30. It took 50 days of waiting from the crucifixion to the coming of the Holy Spirit. There is a "set time" for events to occur.

- Waiting through limbo times is no longer a problem when you have faith without ambiguity and know that God is working "in the meantime."

Watch

The word "watch" *(tsapah)* is found in Hebrew texts about 37 times. The meaning in this context is "to anxiously lean forward with anticipation" with a purpose of seeing. Watching with expectation!

To See, Perceive

Habakkuk stood guard on the rampart watching to *SEE* what God would say. The verb *ra'ah* means, "to perceive, get acquainted with, gain understanding, or examine..."[1] Notice that Habakkuk stands and waits to SEE (or comprehend, not just hear) what is said.

Speak

Here we focus on the content (meaning) of what was said. It was the "word of the Lord" that came to Habakkuk as he stood and waited. The question here is, will you stand and wait until you see what God will say to you?

And the answer? Here it comes in the next verse! Hearing from the Lord gives vision. *"And Jehovah answered me, and said, 'Write the vision,* (write my answer on a billboard) *and make it plain upon tablets* (large and clear), *that he may run that reads it. So that anyone can read it at a glance and rush to tell the others"* (Hab. 2:2).

---

1. All definitions condensed from Vine's Expository Dictionary of Biblical Words, ibid.

Your vision should exceed all your known limitations and boundaries.

Condition yourself for MASSIVE SUCCESS. Look into the promises of heaven and pull those things into the NOW (on earth). See success and not failure. Confess and rehearse limitless possibilities.

"*Life is either a daring adventure or nothing at all.*" Helen Keller

Take a look at yourself in the mirror of your mind and describe what God has created you to look like. As you read this next section, look back at your overall life vision. What would you really want? *THINK BIG!* For example, in five years I will pastor a large church, be a president of a large bank, graduate from High School, become a criminal lawyer, or be able to run a marathon, etc.

Begin to write your over-arching life vision statement here:

Your vision is your MISSION in life. What is the greatest purpose toward which you should direct your efforts and emotions? Tapping into God's intention for your life brings unlimited ENERGY and compelling effectiveness to fulfill that purpose.

State here the vision for your financial future:

I _____(sign your name) have decided to walk in this specific area of faith:_____
_____.

Date_____

MEMORIZE YOUR VISION! I put mine on a video to watch. Allow the Holy Spirit to search your belly for your valid vision.

* What lets you know this is your vision and not what someone else wants for you?

- Do you sense peace and assurance that this is right for you - and not "double mindedness." It is interesting that the root word for the word *double* is *doubt*! Doubt is unbelief.

- Does your vision ignite you? Does it spark your spirit-man?

- Does it press you into increase and tremendous change? It should!

- Can you do this with integrity and honor?

- The right vision will give you passion and demand sacrifice?

- Does it seem impossible? Does it take you far? Is it meaningful? Noble?

CONFESSION: *This VISION is a dream that will come to pass in my life. Therefore, I walk in faith because it pleases God (Heb. 11:6). He rewards my faith with the understanding of His will, by which I will obtain victory.*

I refuse to see, hear, or sense any other negative sense oriented feeling or emotion. I can do whatever God says, therefore, I do not fear failure. I am calm and restful – never anxious or fretful. My soul is prosperous and transformed.

I take the oversight of my life (1 Pet. 5:2). I understand that my vision is not just to do the Word of God, but to become it. SIGNED_____date_____

This activity of writing and/or recording vision develops the reason why you will do something later – it becomes your resolution and conviction – the driving force to your actions.

Always bear in mind that our own resolution to succeed is more important than any other one thing. - Abraham Lincoln

➜ *Your correct vision is God's plan waiting to become a reality.*

Continue to develop your vision. Make it plain.

Say, *"My life is worth living well."*

Day 27 - Focus on your Goals

"If you want to be happy, set a goal that commands your thoughts, liberates your energy, and inspires your hopes."
– Andrew Carnegie

Once you develop the right VISION, you can create productive goals to get there!

 A GOAL is an affirmative, specific, exact, measurable time bound objective toward which you direct an internally fixed, specific sequence of actions that demands commitment and excellent effort until it is accomplished.

"The greatest danger for most of us is not that our aim is too high and we miss it, but that it is too low and we hit it." Michelangelo

A goal is not an ambiguous statement like being "I want to build retirement." A goal aims high and is specific, "I will save $250.00 a month by automatic withdrawal that is put in a Mutual Fund for ten years to use only for my retirement.

GOALS - an acronym

Goals with
Objectives
Assure
Lasting
Success

"It's not enough that we do our best; sometimes we have to do what's required." Sir Winston Churchill

Setting goals is a lifelong process. Every day, each segment of your life's journey should move you toward accomplishing your dreams.

Look again at the overall Vision you wrote for your financial future and decide what BIG projects you need to do to get there.

With this Vision in mind, look back on your list of 8 things that you've been developing and decide if they are really the goals of your life that LEAD TO YOUR OVERALL VISION. (They should be!)

Decide. Make up your mind. Don't spend another moment of your precious time wondering what you want to do. Don't say, "One of these days I'll...." That day will never come. It's time to say, "I'll do it now!"

"The key is not SPENDING time, but in INVESTING it."
Stephen Covey

Having a goal to achieve something is a fantasy until you write it down. Don't for a moment assume that merely "thinking about goals" will allow you to achieve the same benefit. It doesn't work. You simply must WRITE THEM DOWN -- and be very specific. Review and re-establish them monthly.

Look back at your vision and all the things you want to achieve in the future. Say that you want to become a High School gym teacher (or whatever— a financial investor, a preacher, policeman, etc.). That VISION necessitates that you "get ready."

All your goals should reflect and contribute to this authentic over-arching VISION. Once your GOALS are in writing, let the idea be established in your heart. You can expand that concept as you gain clarity.

- Specific goals means that you do fewer useless things.
- Having a goal directed life will bring you prosperity.
- Goals determine how you spend your time.
- Goals determine what you produce.
- Goals allow you to live an astonishing life.

- Your goals should divide your vision into bite sized parts.

- Goals should challenge and energize you to work fast.

- A goal must light your fire, motivate, and excite you.

- They must align to your dreams and creativity.

- They must allow for imagination and creativity.

- The right goals will use your vision, dreams, personality, talents, and even your location. Don't try to be like anyone else – just become the best YOU can be.

- Only 3% of Americans set and follow goals! Yet, specific goals will absolutely enable greater success.

- Confusion and unclear statements cause more underachievement than any other single factor.

- Keep refining your goals to be more specific and clear.

- Goals give guidelines for where to develop your faith.

- Long-term goals cause you to make intelligent decisions.

How will you possess your vision?

Godly goals will include the non-negotiable values that are part of your life. Your goals are THE PLAN and strategy on HOW you will accomplish your vision! You need to develop a solid PLAN to accomplish it. Take action steps to bring your future potential into reality about prosperity.

Examine your list of 8 desires. Use those that align with your vision. The goals you have listed should now affect every decision you make. If your choice doesn't fit with your predetermined life plan, don't DO IT!

There's an old saying that goes, *"If you don't have a goal, it's very unlikely that you will reach it."*

"The plans of the diligent lead to PROFIT as surely as haste leads to poverty." (Prov. 21:5)
Work on DOING your GOAL list!

Every day say, *"My life is worth living well."*

Day 28 - Focus on Plans and Strategies for Deliberate Wealth -

Now that you have your vision and your goals in mind, it is time to strategize a plan for how this is all going to happen.

People are not all automatically blessed financially just because they are Christians. It's about developing the right strategy to get to where you need to go.

You wouldn't walk into a dark bathroom and expect the bathtub to fill by itself. Would you? You need to take some steps to take a bath - there is a small plan. Don't wait around in the dark all your life "hoping" that your tub will fill all by itself!

You must have a plan to make incremental gains to accomplish your vision. Plans may change - but your vision remains stable. Your plan should provide the shortest way to get to your goals. Ask, "How can I get there? What is first?"

Become liberated with the understanding that as you organize and plan, your life automatically becomes managed in ways so that you can achieve your greatest hopes and dreams.

Believe for essential leaps forward!

You must re-frame your strategy and belief system. Everything can be improved upon. Avoid unnecessary routines that just fill your days. Make a strategy that moves you several levels beyond where you are.

You have the same number of hours in a day that Jesus had. He had a plan and knew what to do next. There is right timing in every strategy... be sure to look for it.

You can change your life forever by planning right now on how to maximize your life and talents. Right NOW is the perfect time to empower your life and maximize your future. It's not too late.

Biblical Mindset about Focus and Planning

The blessing of Abraham comes to those in Christ Jesus (Gal. 3:14). *Abraham was RICH in livestock, silver, and gold!* (Gen. 13:2)

The prosperity of the righteous is stable and develops continuously even into old age even when the normal power to make wealth has departed. (Psalm 92:12-14), The prosperity of the righteous cannot be affected by evil. No matter your age – keep on planning!

"The blessing of the LORD brings wealth, and he adds no trouble to it." (Prov. 10:22 NIV)

Be deliberate about following your strategy.

When Uzziah was sixteen, "He SET himself to seek God...and as long as he sought (inquired of, yearned for) the Lord, God made him to PROSPER" (2 Chron. 26:25).

Jesus SET (fixed) His face upon Jerusalem (Lk. 9:51) and didn't deviate from His mission.

You can SET yourself to seek God and prosper. This kind of strategy affects your soul (heart) and determines your future accomplishments, how you feel, and where you go from here.

- You bring forth a good treasure from your own heart (Matt. 12:35, Prov. 23:7).
- A mature believer has his/her heart fixed and doesn't waiver with circumstances (Ps. 108:1).

Once your heart (soul) is "set" (focused), you will rise up and help affect change in your environment and even the next generation. You are a demonstration of God extending the Kingdom.

God shows up when you join His plan.

"Opportunity is missed by most people because it is dressed in overalls and looks like work." Thomas A. Edison

Joseph

Joseph was imprisoned in Egypt. He had no money and no freedom. But, even as a slave, Joseph's soul prospered. He had the ability to make his master rich and therefore was appointed to be in charge of all the Pharaoh's possessions.

Joseph had two sons. The firstborn was Manasseh (who's name means "Forgetting the past"). His second son Ephraim (DOUBLE PROSPERITY), saying, "God has prospe*red me in the land of my sorrow*" (Gen. 41:50 MSG). It's time for you now. Make the most of every day. Forget the past and receive that DOUBLE PORTION!

Nehemiah

Nehemiah was a trusted servant and advisor for King Artaxerxes I (the Persian ruler). Nehemiah lived when the Jews were still in exile. It was Nehemiah's VISION to rebuild Jerusalem and the walls of the city that were still in shambles.

Nehemiah prayed and obtained the permission from King Artaxerxes to begin to rebuild the city (he received spiritual instruction and then made the plan to make it happen). In spite of severe obstacles, Nehemiah was able to finish the job in just 52 days! How did he do it? Nehemiah had goals and then made strategic plans.

- Nehemiah saw the need (Neh. 1:2-4). He asked questions and became informed. His entire mission was based on the Scriptures he found that contained God's promises.

- He prayed (1:4-11). In consecration, he dedicated himself to the purpose and plan of God.

- Nehemiah clearly saw the vision (2:5) and considered the scope of the project. He committed to finish the work.

- He turned the need into an opportunity. He had vision and set goals of what needed to be accomplished and when.

- The plan involved evaluating what was needed (2:5-16). He proactively analyzed the situation and objectively handled the responsibility. He gathered information, material, and money.

- He organized the steps (3:1-32), defined the GOALS, and set the target dates (Neh. 2:5, 6).

- He led, assigned tasks and he communicated vision (2:17-18). He inspected progress.

Thinking Like an Entrepreneur.

What can you DO that will strategically move you forward? Success is your choice. You decide what you are supposed to do, why you want it, and how you can achieve it. No one else could, would, or should do that for you. Plan your life.

God has a plan for you – at your age and at this time.

Success is a choice. Taking action without planning is the main reason for most failure. With a plan to guide you, you can figure out how to get where you are going.

Proper planning, preparation, and scheduling ALWAYS prevents mistakes. You can begin to add your plan to the goal lists in the back. Also, plan each day. Know WHY that action is critical and HOW and WHEN you will do it. Correct decisions come from focusing on your predefined plans.

Life cannot go according to plan, if you don't have a plan and work it!

"Remember this-that there is a proper dignity and proportion to be observed in the performance of every act of life."
Marcus Aurelius Antoninus

The Telegraph (UK newspaper), reported how scientists suggest that the handling of money could prevent or cure pain. Researchers at the University of Minnesota studied patients with chronic pain who counted money before taking part in an experiment and discovered that they experienced lower levels of pain and discomfort than those who did not count money! Their conclusion was that the "fondling paper currency and coins helped ward off pain by boosting feelings of self-worth and self-sufficiency."

Work on DOING your list! Say, "My life is worth living well."

Day 29 - Focus on Prosperous Priorities

Prioritize

Once you have set your goals, you must set the priority in which they need to be accomplished.

Priorities are a huge KEY in learning to prosper. You must determine to choose what you must accomplish NEXT. Decide the tasks that will move you forward to get more accomplished each day. It is a stress reliever to know every day what you need to do first and then next. Much of our time and anxiety could be saved if we FIRST established where we are going and when.

Prior = earlier in time or order, something that takes precedence. What is more important than other things. Here the objective is *not what you want to do* – but *what you need to do next.*

Pick your priorities - don't try to do too much. Eliminate unnecessary actions. Separate the "good" from the "right." What is absolutely necessary? What can you do later? In your free time? What can be delegated? What takes up all your time? Eliminate all habitual busy work and obligatory functions that you really don't have to do.

"The wisdom of life consists in the elimination of non-essentials."
Lin Yutang

All facets of your life must be worked in harmonious synchronization with your overall VISION. All your goals should link together to accomplish the greater long-range PURPOSE.

Exceptions!

Sometimes, we need to do more than one thing at a time! The experts say, "Put God first, then everything else falls in line..."

144

They say to put family second, church third, job fourth. But we all know that's impossible. What about single people? Do they just omit that second spot of family? Or have no second?

How can we prioritize work after church? Many times it is impossible to try to compartmentalize our lives and set our priorities in a one-two three four list. And where do your dreams come in? Only if the other areas are finished? Of course not. Life can't be a continual balancing act where the juggler continually races to not miss catching a spinning plate.

A list of sequential priorities doesn't always make sense - sometimes we have to work on more than one step at the SAME TIME. You can have three or four "nexts!"

THE GREAT COMMISSION: Jesus told us in Matthew 22:34-40 that the greatest commandment (singular) was to love God, and then your neighbor as yourself. We understand that the two segments of this commandment aren't listed in a ranked order, but rather these two commandments link together as being of coequal and corresponding significance.

The "second is likened to the first..." constituting the essence of the law. Though different in direction, they are seen as equal in importance. "On these two commandments *depend* the whole law and the prophets."

- *DEPEND* (in this reference) means to suspend or hold in place. These two commandments are the hook from which the entire Old Testament suspends. Here we have a complete statement of what is important in life. The second portion of the commandment is not of secondary importance (it is like (equal to) the first).

It's not always doing this first, and then do this second -- but to do both AT THE SAME TIME is the minimum required. Keeping the centrality of God and your fellow man in your every plan allows the Holy Spirit to touch you in every arena of your life.

You must do THREE things at the same time. Love God. Love your fellowman. And love yourself. Yes. You have to give yourself the permission to love yourself! That's a priority of the Great Commission! All at the same time...

In order to accomplish your vision, you must assign top priorities in your life, your job, your plans, and your responsibilities. All your thoughts and plans must combine to make certain that you love God, others, AND yourself!

- You can't fully love God until you know Him and trust Him.

- You can't love others until you really know them, and that takes effort. You must value them and appreciate them to love them. You must relate to them and communicate.

- You can't really love yourself until you know who you are IN GOD. That's why we started this book learning this very same Scripture about loving yourself.

So in fulfilling this commandment, you must also see that all your primary goals are strategically co-related and significant to accomplishing the overall plan.

 It may be easier for you to think of these top priorities of your vision as being in a circle rotating around your spiritual center and joined by prayer. Being center means that the nucleus of your life is God, and all else revolves around that concept. God gives purpose to all other things that you do. Choose activities that co-ordinate and move you towards your Godly VISION.

Prioritizing saves time.

Each goal has numerous steps that need to be prioritized. You don't need to spend the same amount of time on each goal. For example, let's choose a possible goal to build retirement. This goal may have a different series of STEPS for each person - but those steps are mandatory to achieve that objective. Write down the action steps of what needs to happen to accomplish this task in the most effective manner. (i.e. Build retirement).

1. Hire work assistant.

2. Find outsourcing help.

3. Don't eat out as much.

4. Learn about investments. Real Estate. Stocks.

5. Research savings opportunities. Put savings on autopilot.

6. Search for new ideas to make money.

7. File all receipts by category for tax savings.

8. Automate your bill paying.

9. Learn to schedule better. Use a planner - don't try to remember everything that needs to be done.

10. Get a good money program to keep track (Quicken).

11. Use over-draft protection that won't generate extra charges.

12. Hire a Financial Planner.

13. Get ready. Order your days. Prioritize your time.

14. Clear all debt. Owe no man anything.

15. Win the lottery. (Just checking if you are reading this.)

16. Develop strategic strategy.

"The greatest invention in the world is compound interest!"
Albert Einstein

Simply decide which **STEPS** are most important, and then order (prioritize) the list. You may choose first to hire a personal assistant because that would free you up to do more business and earn more money than you could gain by saving for retirement at this point.

 Focus immediately on the highest priority goals and the highest step needed. Direct all of your attention on those imperative first steps.

Every day say, "My life is worth living well."

CONFESSION: *"Everything that I need has already been given."*

Day 30 - Focus On Change

By now you may realize that God is willing to prosper you. But you may not know HOW He's going to do it! Maybe you're still expecting someone to leave a basket on your front doorstep just loaded with cash!

Fantasy expectations always leave you disappointed. Immature presumptions immobilize you. Feelings of entitlement never go very far. Feeling like you "deserve it," never work!

Focusing on your circumstances about the lack of money won't make you any more money (anymore that focusing on disease won't heal your disease). Limiting beliefs and negativity are destructive and powerful habits.

Do you know WHY you have nonproductive habits? You must challenge what you believe and expect. There are solutions. Don't give room for doubt any longer. Your beliefs should not hold you back but they should move you forward. Focus on what works. Decide to RUN!

Correct beliefs and positive thinking always lead to correct actions.

Deliberate Change

"Progress is impossible without change, and those who cannot change their minds, cannot change anything."
George Bernard Shaw

Now that you are gaining insight, consider the things you need to CHANGE to optimize your future and cause your dreams to become a reality.

If you are addicted to your old traditional ways of doing things you won't be able to get there! You must continually be in the process of change to new productive habits.

To become prosperous, YOU must do things differently.

Nobody really likes to change! And most of the time, the process of change is unnerving! But remember, the only constant in the world is change. It must be a constant cycle of re-inventing yourself to keep relevant.

"The first and best victory is to conquer self." Plato

"God grant me the wisdom to know I can change ME."

Change is everywhere. Change is the path to expansion. It is where you replace worn-out beliefs with more extended and elevated ones. Greater personal self-expression comes as you learn to continually transition into new realms (from glory to Glory, from faith to Faith).

What Should You CHANGE? Ask yourself:

- What attitudes do I want to reflect to others?
- What do I need to remove from my life?
- What is no longer productive? What can I eliminate?
- What are the time killers?
- What can I do differently?
- How can I connect to my life's assignment without incorporating the old musty paradigms?

"First say to yourself what you would be; and then DO what you have to do." Epictetus

CONFESSION: *I'm willing to change now - even if I don't know what to do next, I'm open to change. I'm taking that leap of faith that will lead to abundance!*

It's not just a changed life that you want, but a totally exchanged life.

 Has it ever occurred to you to ask God to give you a bigger vision? To give you greater favor? To show you how to walk in supernatural wisdom? Has it dawned on you that your success is a great and influential tool to reach the lost?

- Jacob would not let go of the angel until he was blessed!

- Jabez wanted enlarged territory.

- Ask! Instead of viewing your life as wishful thinking, view these thoughts as seeds to be planted.

Growth demands change.

To change your life demands that you exchange your life for His. You take up God's plans. You build His Kingdom. The job of the Holy Spirit is to GUIDE AND CHANGE YOU. He leads you as a spiritual person who is moving toward greater spiritual realization. He also leads you as to how to manage your existence on earth.

God gives you in life what you are able to MANAGE!

Managing Your Changed Life

The management of your changed life gives you dominion success.

Leap forward to your potential. Assume that for you there are no limitations anymore. There are no limits for your life except for those you accept. Your beliefs and thoughts are what limit your future.

> Only you can change YOU or re-invent YOURSELF.

Are you ready to DESIGN a better life?
Change your conversation? Change your behavior? Change who you think you are? Move fast! Work on DOING your list!

Did you remember to be grateful?

Every day say, *"My life is worth living well."*

Day 31 -Focus on Finishing

You must finish! What gets in the way? When you know your reasons for procrastination, you can address the issues that stop your progress!

1. Overwhelmed? Is The task Is Too Big?

An old joke asks, "How do you eat an elephant?" Answer, "One bite at a time." It's a "divide and conquer solution." Many goals must be broken down into manageable smaller incremental steps. Conquer each task, one at a time. Define natural milestones inside each project.

Each large goal consists of strategic plans that entail a lot of small tasks. Need to lose 80 pounds? Go for 20 pounds, 4 times! Need to clean the basement? Break it down to North, South, East, and West. Or divide your project into certain time constraints every day (15 minutes, 1 hour, etc). Get help. Eventually you will finish a large task and be able to move on to the next one.

2. Fear The End Result Won't Be What You Want?

We fear failure and we fear success. Fear is:
False
Evidence
Appearing
Real.

Fears are like small kids - the ones that scream the loudest get the most attention. Fear distracts.

3. The Task Is Boring?

It's easy to get caught up in details and forget 'WHY' you are doing it. Whether it is cleaning the garage or making phone calls... focus on the bigger picture. Remember your WHY.

4. Indecision?

If you can't decide, move on to the next task.

5. You Lack Ability?

Easy. Find out where to gain the skills you need or find someone with the right skills who can help you.

6. Distracted?

Distractions always seem to be a 'good' reason not to get something done. Try turning off the telephone, turning off your e-mail, and just focusing on what needs to happen.

7. Trying To Do Too Many Things?

Do you focus too much on what is unimportant? You must learn to focus on the predetermined important assignments -- and not be distracted by the urgent demands of life. (Cares of this world can choke out the Word (Matt. 13:22).

8. Unable To Choose?

God often allows us to start out going one direction and then, as we move along, He may turn us around and go another way. He'll tell us early if we listen! Paul was on his way to Macedonia when the Spirit of the Lord gave him instructions to go another way (Acts 16:1-9).

Balaam is another example: He's just going along and suddenly, the donkey simply lies down, because that's all she can do. The donkey saw that it was the wrong way.

Trust that God will lead you or change your direction!

Pay attention to what your brain wants to think about and then forcibly exercise the discipline of focusing on the Goodness of God and His blessings in your life.

Take some time today to consider HOW to expand the influence of your life. Write down your thoughts.

What kind of income do you desire to make next year?

Now...double that goal right now. Impossible? Good. That's a good place to be. Identify this set point of your present belief system- that is outside the realm of what you believe. Write and speak confessions into this resistance. God can do above all that YOU can ever ask or think (Eph. 3:20),.

Success means that you set obtainable objectives in each category of life.

- Know you can prosper.

- Determine you will prosper.

- Make an action plan and DO IT!

- Do certain things every day that must be done (have a routine). Soon, you will be amazed at your achievements!

Detail Your Goals and Design a Better Life.

Look back at your developing list of 8 things you want. This should now be your goal list. Now, GO TO THE BACK OF THIS BOOK AND PUT ONE GOAL ON the top of EACH GOAL SHEET, etc. Include your action verbs, priorities, enthusiasm, creativity, etc.

Right goals move your dreams and wishes into realities.

WHAT: Write precise objective: (*increase income by $2,000. Be my own boss, etc*).

HOW: (*Mentors, training needed, costs, etc.*).

WHY: (*Go back and check your WHYs*).

WHEN: (*By Dec. 31, 20__*). Set Deadlines to complete each goal.

- WHEN makes the idea become a tangible goal. Setting deadlines causes you to optimize your time and not get distracted. Determine exactly how you will measure your progress.

- By answering WHEN! You must have and keep deadlines.

- Intentionally insist on internally fixed deadlines and finishing assignments. Make appointments with yourself.

- Deadlines enforce self-accountability. Always put a when!

- WHENs improve results, create energy and efficiency. WHENs challenge to get it done!

- WHENs have realistic deadlines.

The old saying is true - *Everything takes as long as you allow!*

You MUST review these deadlines every month!

Review is what keeps you on track. If you don't review, you will be seriously disappointed in your results. Review is essential and will become natural. Try reviewing on the 1st of every month.

Write your favorite prosperity Scriptures on 3X5 cards.

- Read these cards before going to bed at night.

- Take time to visualize what success and favor looks like.

- Place these cards in your car, at your office, your refrigerator, and especially on your bathroom mirror.

- Remember to keep speaking out loud continually so that you can hear yourself make correct affirmations.

   There is a part of your brain that thrives on subconsciously considering and working on significant tasks. This subconscious reality will really make a difference. Your subconscious works on these goals ALL THE TIME.

Wealth isn't just money, because money can't bring you every happiness. It is prosperity to be fulfilled while enjoying your life. It is being at peace with your life, your family, and your work.

Lasting prosperity comes only by purposeful, planned, and deliberate thought and action. Begin today to list everything you need to do the next day... this is an effective way to invoke the LAW OF PROSEPRITY. Focus your daily attention on what comes next. By simply considering your next steps and strategies for that new day, you gain control of your life and energy. You give yourself a new lease on life – and... the unparalleled gift of LIFE.

CONFESSIONS:
CONFESSION: *"I am handpicked by God to live at this moment in time. I can make right decisions and overcome any barrier and succeed to fulfill my destiny. "*

"I will overcome all adverse reactions to negative influences and negative words. I believe for the impossible and embrace every opportunity for the miraculous! I'm strengthened by Godly promises to make an IMPACT in this lifetime."

What are you grateful for?

Work on DOING your list you are building in the back!

Every day say, *"My life is worth living well."*

40 Days
on
Prosperity

Section #7, Understanding & Application

Your Melchizedek Priesthood

Money and Prosperity

Living in Prosperity

Having a Business

Day 32 - Focus on Your Melchizedek Priesthood of Prosperity

Biblical Mindset

Right from the start, God's purpose was to build His Kingdom on the earth with humans. In fact, He gave us the order to rule (Gen. 1:26). Truly, He had decided that this Kingdom was ours even before he made the earth...

Humans found it difficult to believe that they could rule the earth. They fell from grace and later they forgot their Garden mandate. Moses came down from the mountain to tell them about being Kings and Priests, but they would not respond. The Levitical priesthood was established instead of God's intention.

Hebrews tells us that the "priesthood changed" (Heb. 7:12)! Jesus brought a new priesthood. Many modern churches fail to realize the fact that we don't exist under the old Levitical order of things any more! Jesus intended us to have a Melchizedek Priesthood – one charged with the power of eternal life.

This Melchizedek rule can be fully expressed in you. Your Biblical worldview must include the inheritance of this new royal priesthood. Melchizedek: is both a priest and a King

Greek as a language is abstract, but Hebrew's words are full of the nitty-gritty of daily life. They embrace ideas that can be applied here and now, to what life really means.

When broken down, the Hebrew word Melchizedek (Gen. 7:1) is comprised of two parts. The first, *melch*, means "king." A King rules over his kingdom, or a jurisdiction or dominion.[1]

If we are under Melchizedek, we then asked the question, WHERE do WE RULE? WHAT do we rule over?

Melchizedek's rule was of a specific KINGDOM of *tsedek* (or the second half of his name). Most of the time when translated, *tsedek*, (*tsdeq, zedeq*) approximates either "RIGHTEOUSNESS" or "JUSTICE." However, if we did further, we see that there's much more meaning to it.

Tsedeq comes from a Semitic word meaning to be firm, straight, "like steel," a determined integrity that goes to one's core. In Arabic, this means that one is fully developed, balanced and mature.

Although *tsedeq* is often translated to mean "judgment," this does not mean evil retribution or a legal kind of judgment. Believers can take heart because God's *Tsedeq* (justice and righteousness) also incorporates RIGHT LIVING, equity, bounty, health and prosperity.

Stated most clearly, the literal of *tsedeq* means that one is to rule and live a LIFE of full PROSPERITY and BALANCE. *Tsedeq* is the energy that brings all things into right alignment, into the created order. Therefore, the Melchizedek priesthood allows you to totally rule over PROSPERITY (wholeness, fullness and finances), which in turn balances the world.

We can be KINGS OF PROSPERITY

---

1. See my book, "King Priest" for details.

If one is to have real Melchizedek PROSPERITY, it must be demonstrated and taught. It does not mean a poverty of spirit with religious justification. This causes the Church to be all the more self-involved and focused on problems.

Tsedeq as prosperity, balance, health, maturity and right living, is our domain and must become so. This is the land we rule. If the method of our authority and rule is not firmly rooted in *tsedeq*, we have not fully entered our dominion.

God manages things with *tsedeq* (Ps 96:11). Think about that for a minute. The LORD God told Abraham, "Find me 10 righteous (*tsedeq*), and I will rescue Sodom." However, not even ten in Sodom were living their lives as fully balanced and mature beings. Not 10 in the whole city truly understood that prosperity at home this could be theirs. The question is, are there ten righteous now - today?

Friends, Jesus, gives you His priesthood, which in turn allows you to rule a prosperous and balanced dominion. This is how you influence the world with rule and how you can influence the world globally. This is our sign of strength -- and how you can effectively move to occupy territories.

As you RULE the earth in Melchizedek prosperity, you mandate heaven's rule.

- God said that humans should rule the earth.

- Jesus became your *tsedeq* and reconciled you back.

- You awaken that skill to rule with *tsedeq* (prosperity, balance and maturity) with your faith.

- God's Kingdom is within you and expands according to the amount of rule you are given.

- Jesus waits in heaven until all things are restored (rule of dominion).

- As His Kingdom rule commences on earth, His return will come more quickly.

What are you grateful for?   Work on DOING your list!

Day 33 - Focus on Money and Prosperity

"Money is like manure. It isn't worth a thing unless it's spread around encouraging young things to grow!" Thornton Wilder

Until this present day, you have either exceeded your expectations of what you thought you could achieve. Regardless of where you currently are, with the correct strategy, you CAN have greater success... soon!

Most research indicates a strong relationship between happiness and success. That doesn't mean that money can buy happiness, but when you begin to see that your aspirations can be accomplished, you do have a greater sense of contentment and joy.

Keep in mind that the purpose of prosperity should be viewed as a means of accomplishing something. Because our personality, gifts, and talents are diverse, we all see different objectives.

MONEY IS IMPORTANT

Ask, "Why do I want more money?" Give the real answer, not just a religious one that sounds good.

HOW can money help you achieve your overall vision?

Describe in detail your first memory about money?

Who first told you about money? Were they rich or poor? How did they relate to you?

How and when did you first earn money?

How did your parents relate to money?

Did you get an allowance? Did you work for it? Did you appreciate getting it? How did you spend it?

Did you ever lose money making a bad decision? How did it make you feel?

What is your past record about financial responsibility?

What's important about money? Money is neutral – it can be used for good and bad. Money can be a symbol that allows you to interact in exchange. It can solve specific problems. Desiring money is not the same thing as being greedy!

King Solomon said that "Money answers ALL things" (Ecc. 10:19). It does seem to help out a lot. It allows you to build the Kingdom and expand the influence of good in the world. You can help others. Bring education, and improvements. You can enjoy

and posses many good things in life. It allows you to create your future and create inheritance for your children's children (Prov. 13:22).

The European ruler, Napoleon was asked, "What are the three most essential requisites in war?" He answered, *"The first is money; the second is money; and the third is money."*

The Bible is full of people who knew how to manage and use wealth properly. The ancient Bible character Job is one of the best examples of Biblical prosperity. Before his testings, his possessions were seven thousand sheep, three thousand camels, five hundred yoke of oxen, five hundred female donkeys, and a very large household. After his trial ended, his possessions doubled.

Abraham was "very rich" in cattle, silver, and gold (Gen. 13:2). He owned over 300 trained warrior servants. David was also incredibly rich.

Solomon was said to surpass all the kings who ever lived in riches and wisdom. He had 12,000 horses and owned so much silver it was just like an ordinary rock (2 Chron. 9:27).

Joseph ruled in Egypt as the minister of the Pharaoh's money!

The Queen of Sheba had an entourage caring for her belongings. The virtuous woman is praised for her remarkable abilities in trade, real estate, and investments (Prov.31). She, of course, is a symbol of the Church.

And yet, many think that Jesus was poor. But remember, when He was born, the Magi brought gold, frankincense, and myrrh - which were very precious. Jesus was a carpenter and knew how to provide for Himself. He brought along a personal accountant (the treasurer Judas). Their treasury seems to have been large enough that nobody noticed when Judas took 30 pieces of silver. Jesus wore a seamless robe that had such value that at the cross, the Roman soldiers gambled for it.

Focusing on Facts or Truth

Much of our financial and economic structures are failing and in deep trouble. Unfortunate news is all around us.

It is a **FACT** that in the midst of winter, all the trees appear to be dead - but the truth is that inside that tree life continues churning and awaiting the right moment to emerge.

> **FACTS are not always the TRUTH of reality!**

Whenever you are faced with what seems to be "the facts," you must try to find the true reality that is concealed within those facts. Seeing reality (Scriptural truth) inside the "facts" of this world is a huge key to your success. You don't need to worry about news.

FACT: Economic times are difficult.

TRUTH: There are many, even in this difficult economic time, who are prospering and thriving. Who's report will you believe? (Rom. 10:16)

No matter what happens in the news... there are massively wonderful opportunities in the world today - for YOU. Everyone has their own belief systems and everyone has their own economic outlook! You are not controlled by the stock market or the daily news!

The present economic condition of the world is not "personal" or even about you. It's imperative that you turn from any fear and focus your thoughts on positive action.

Looking at **FACTS** can cause double-mindedness. The reason why people change their mind is because they aren't sure they made the right choice in the first place. They look at other people – they read about other people's problems – and they change their minds.

What are your current worries concerning money?

Write what the lack of money has caused you to do and feel:

(For example, do you want to hoard and be a pack rat unable to throw things away? Do you live with clutter, unable to dispose of it?)

The truth is that IF we apply Kingdom principles in our lives, we will find success. We have been given every spiritual blessing in heavenly places in Christ in order to influence our world. Double mindedness stops forward momentum. BEING-ness is the faculty of choice. Single-minded choices are the directed and intentional decisions you make that shape your future.

Focus means you bring concentration to a central point, having a sense of certainty and clarity, so that you can make a firm decision.

Success demands that you narrow down the arena of possibilities in order to determine a single choice.

"Since a dull ax requires great strength, sharpen the blade. That's the value of wisdom; it helps you succeed!" (Ecc. 10:10).

Every day say, *"My life is worth living well."*

What are you grateful for?

Day 34 - Focus on Living Prosperously

Imagine yourself in the future - after you've transformed into that next-level person. Try to see the way you look and the way you look at others. See how you are settled and efficient. Notice how things are organized, planned, and structured with purpose. Imagine energy and optimism. Allow yourself to look through this new "lens" of faith, assurance, and possibility.

Ruling and reigning over your life and future expresses that you are real sons and daughters of the Lord God and that you are created in His true image.

How do you behave around people who have lots of money?

How do you feel when you spend lots of money?

Do you feel ashamed of how you spend it? Do you feel awkward when you talk about money?

What does your subconscious feel about being wealthy?

As long as your OLD identity holds you in limitation, you will never operate in revelation understanding that releases the NEW.

You may outwardly think you want prosperity and yet inwardly resist. Any internal resistance prevents God's blessings to flow to you. Poverty thinking will totally derail you.

"Wisdom is better than strength. But the poor man's wisdom is despised, and his words are no longer heeded." (Ecc. 9:16).

Did you read that Scripture? A poor man's words are NOT heeded. Nobody should take financial advice from a poor person!

Have you noticed how poor people generally spend their money on low quality things just because they are less expensive? They are afraid to get something of value, even though the cheaper things won't last. Soon, they become dissatisfied with the inferior quality and realize that they just wasted their money. Unhappiness with bargain purchases just amplifies the poverty mindset. In actuality, they create greater poverty.

The more dilapidated stuff you hoard around you, the more your subconscious mind holds onto poverty. We're not talking about overspending or getting into debt. We're talking about improving your surroundings as you can.

We are learning how the poor generally think and act differently than the rich. Poor people tend to think more narrowly and with more limited perceptions – they fear flowing with new ideas! Generally, the poor work for someone else. They don't recognize the right decisions. They do things ordinarily and routinely. Often the poor are harder workers.

Poor people communicate scarcity while rich people communicate plenty.

Poor people tend to think about themselves first, while rich people tend to think of others first.

Fact is: It's not easy for a poor person to become wealthy but it's very simple for a rich person to gain wealth. That's because the poor person has a limited mind-set while the rich are more creative and expansive with their ideas. It's true - the rich get richer and the poor get poorer!

Dishonest money dwindles away but he who gathers money little by little makes it grow" (Prov. 13:11).

The Love of Money -

"The lack of money is the root of all evil!" George Bernard Shaw

One of the most misunderstood Scriptures is, "the LOVE OF MONEY IS THE ROOT OF ALL EVIL" (1 Tim. 6:10). Many denominations use this particular Scripture to validate their poverty stance.

However, the word "love" (*philaguria*) *does NOT translate* THE "LOVE" of money - BUT being "GREEDY OR STINGY!" This translation should read, "For BEING GREEDY with money is a root of all kinds of bad things." Coveting (the Biblical term for lust and greed) is indeed the root of most human sin.

> Proverbs 28:22 enhances this translations, "A stingy man is eager to get rich and is unaware that poverty awaits him." Sometimes, everyone is stingy in one way or another and we must examine our motives and decisions.

This Scripture doesn't condemn the acquisition of money or wealth. In fact, it is God Who gives you prosperity.

We are clearly told what brings poverty:

- "He who loves pleasure becomes poor" (Prov. 21:17),

- "A person of perverse thought won't prosper" (Prov. 17:2).

- "He who works will have abundant food, but the one who chases fantasies will have his fill of poverty!" (Prov. 28:19).

- "How long will you lie there you sluggard? A little sleep, a little slumber, a little folding of the hands to rest and poverty will come unto you like a bandit" (Prov. 6:9-11).

- Because you did not serve the Lord joyfully and gladly in the time of prosperity, therefore in hunger and thirst, in nakedness and dire poverty, you will serve the enemies that the Lord sends against you" (Deut. 28:47-48).

"Money is the answer to everything!" Ecc. 10:19

ATTITUDES TO MOVE FORWARD: You may not be able to avoid some of the obvious signs of poverty yet, but you can begin to establish a prosperity consciousness.

- Always live within your current means of income.

- As your situation improves, you can gradually remove the poverty in your life, and replace it with things you really want and need.

- Refuse to allow yourself to have a poverty mind-set - no matter what your situation. Don't give off conflicting signals. Remove all signs of poverty THINKING and your reality will change. It will!

- Take care of your money and your things with respect and appreciation.

- Speak the affirmation, "Money comes to me for what I do!" "People love to give to me!"

- You don't "lay up treasure on earth," but you can enjoy what you have while you are here.

- Believe it when you say, "I'm worth it!"

- Let affirming words echo into your mind and create new pathways of possibility. Life and death really are in the tongue (Prov. 18:21).

- Learn to feel good about the possessions that you already have - not guilty. Feel good. Look good.

- Make your home as beautiful as you can and enjoy it. Even if you have to sweep up your dirt floor for now, make it nice!

- Look at your bank account and realize that it will change.

- Imagine and visualize prosperity coming into your life.

- When you do actually get some money, don't just go out and spend it right away. Give yourself a chance to consider the best options for using it! You can have money without being attached to it.

- And, don't worry - if you lose it all, it can come back to you a hundred-fold.

I have a friend who named her two dogs, "Money" and "Debt Free!" When she calls them she says, "Money, come!" She knows that her words matter and that she can speak prosperity into her situations.

We started out this book talking about the co-existing beauties of spiritual realities becoming tangible on earth. When you call (pray, declare, proclaim) the heavenly to materialize tangibly here - upon earth, they both really are the same things. Both spiritual and tangible come from God - the Source of energy.

Continue working on your goals at the back of the book. Try to put them in prioritized order.

When you get this all finished, copy your top 8 goals on 3X5 cards and laminate this card to carry with the Scripture card you made yesterday. Read both cards before every meal and before you go to bed. Constantly remind yourself of what needs to happen next.

Begin to think about your NEXT project in LIFE.

What are you grateful for?

Work on DOING your list of 8 things! Live the LIFE you were meant to live - and DO IT NOW with purposeful action.

Every day say, "My life is worth living well."

CONFESSION: *"The same power that rose Jesus from the dead now quickens (enlivens, activates, energizes) me in my mortal body!"*

Day 35 - Focus on Managing

You can "learn" to manage what comes your way. Like we've mentioned, change often causes resistance and blockage even against what you really want. You need to solve problems and manage every resistance.

- Begin to reinvent how you do things. How can you improve what you are doing right now?

- Be adaptable - think on your feet!

- Improve and expedite the way you do something.

- Everyday, do what you can steadily do without stress.

- Expect that revelation of all kinds awaits your open understanding!

"Be diligent in these matters; give yourself wholly to them, so that everyone may see your progress" (1 Tim. 4:15 NIV).

You have done all the exercises up to now in order to learn to manage and plan your life. It is time for you to step onto the path of your own specific and unique destiny. The more you expect, the greater your potential. It's not about "having a business" it is about BEING your business.

Today's assignment is to look at every aspect in the framework of your overall vision, dream, talents, and passion that you have already determined. Read back at what you have already decided. Anticipate.

Self actualization begins to have answers: Why were you born? What do you want to do with your life and what do you want to leave behind? Can your life impact future generations? What type of parents should your grandchildren be?

How much do you want to earn, save and invest?

Develop a specific overarching statement that includes the most important points in your life about prosperity.

"No one could make a greater mistake than he who did nothing because he could do only a little."-- Edmund Burke

Biblical prosperity has to do with consistently (habitually) invest wisely (Mat. 25:27), to be shrewd in our business dealings (Luke 16:8), to save for our future generations (Prov. 13:22), and to create business plans (Luke 14:28). The Bible also says to not co-sign for those you do not know well (Prov. 11:15) and to deal honestly with others (Prov. 11:1).

"Good planning and hard work lead to prosperity, but hasty shortcuts lead to poverty" (Prov. 21:5 NLT).

- Pay off all high interest debt first (cars, credit cards, etc.). *"Keep out of debt and own no man anything, except to love one another..."* (Rom. 13:8 AMP).

- Pay off any non tax deductible debts (that you can't write off).

- Finish paying off your mortgage (www.investopedia).

- Collect your tax records all year long and keep them ready.

- Sign up for automatic IRA contributions deducted by bank each month.

- Compare insurance premiums (auto and home).

- Do inventory on assets and get homeowner's insurance.

- Build a Procedures Manual to reproduce your efforts.

As you work with others and build routine tasks, write out every detail of every process in a procedures manual so that someone else can do that job for you the next time.

Detail your protocol and expectation. Teach others how to reproduce what you do so that you can move forward.

Business

Jesus said, "I must be about my Father's "business." Perhaps this *business* could mean more than we first thought! Business can be spiritual! It also can be a Kingdom reality on earth.

> *"We beseech you, brethren, that you increase more and more; and that you study to be quiet, TO DO YOUR OWN BUSINESS, and to work with your own hands as we commanded you that you may walk honestly toward them that are without; and that YOU MAY HAVE LACK OF NOTHING"* (1 Thes. 4:10-12).

A big part of the job of the Church should be to help bring people out of habitual poverty and mediocre mindsets. Too many people don't realize their capacity for business.

Most everyone can manage a small business, even on the side. It's a great idea for every nurse, preacher, or teacher to consider having additional alternative income sources.

Notice this, in everything you do, you are one spirit (1 Cor. 6:17) in the presentation of Christ in the earth! We bring the spiritual to the temporal - God's Kingdom comes on earth as it is in heaven.

Abundance is a conscious alertness of what God has already given.

Building equity in something you own is one of the best choices. You must synchronize your business with:

- What you desire?

- What you love to do?

- What people need and want?

Consider the main points of Paul Getty's book, "How to be Rich."

- Find what you were born to do and enjoy it.
- Almost without exception, there is only one way to make big money - and that is to own your own business.
- The goal of business should be to provide more and better products and services at a lower price.
- Look for legitimate opportunities for expansion.
- Always try to improve your product.
- Take risks. Seek new horizons and untapped markets.
- Build a good reputation.
- Learn SPECIALIZED skills and become proficient.
- Live with discipline and external appointments and deadlines.
- Save money.
- Every business must solve problems! Train yourself to find strategies and SOLUTIONS.
- Have a primary focus and also multiple streams of income.
- Make business decisions, not emotional or ego decisions.
- There are NO LIMITS to what you can do...
- Do certain things every day to EARN money.
- If your present plan isn't working - choose another.

Obviously, having your own business requires working hard and learning how to do it well. It means learning how to manage what you have, how to hire the best, how to delegate, outsource, how to generate income, how to advertise, how to invest money where it appreciates and multiplies the most, and how to disciple and teach others how to gain wealth for kingdom enterprise.

Brainstorm on how you could possibly turn what you love to do into your own business?

Are there options to what you are doing now?

Could a new business be beneficial?

Formulate the question, Should I _____ or _____?

Your DNA is programmed to achieve.

Consider how having a Personal Business gives you flexibility to decide your own schedule and to not work in set environments. Plus tax advantages give you much more spendable income.

Just release your mind to ALL the possibilities in your life. Visualize EVERYTHING you want, write your ideas down. Don't judge yourself for wanting things. Just write. Think like a kid... and ask, ask, ask, ask! Think about the Blessing!

Things to remember about having a business:

- Make sure that you can deliver on what you promise.

- Exceed all expectations.

- Stay in touch.

- Accomplish tasks on time!

- Use STRONG IDEALS, affirmative outlook, confident words, positive thoughts and dream big.

- See your future as finished - and you are being led to the finished place. Watch Olympic champions and how they see their performance ahead of time. Expect to do well.

What are you grateful for?

Every day say, "My life is worth living well."

40 Days on Prosperity

Section #8, "Your Establishment"

Counsel

Reaping

Giving

Establishing

The Finish Line

Day 36 - Focus on Prosperous Counsel!

"Without counsel, plans go awry, but in the multitude of counselors they are established" (Prov. 15:22 NKJV), Don't go it alone!

Write your ideas about WHY you should seek advice about prosperity from those who have already succeeded.

You need to learn from others who have already made the journey! Find out their perspectives. When you have gone as far as you can go, learn to leverage from the experience of experts.

Make a list of successful people who could help you.

What questions could you ask them that would really help?

Formulate specific and focused questions on what is needed to get to where you want to be. Ask bold questions and take bold actions.

You don't need to reinvent the wheel. Find coaches and encouragers whom you can trust. This list may include family, friends, co-workers and whomever else you choose. You can't jump start yourself! You need others to help you out. Good connections bring greater energy. Be teachable! Don't talk all the time - LISTEN.

 Look for connections (jumper cables) where you can maintain individuality and individual expression that is combined with accountable inter-dependence.

This is a huge lesson to learn: You need to rally strong people around and recognize their value to your life. God's plan for your life includes OTHER people to help jump start you to success.

Find those who will be a blessing to you and who will be totally honest. "... *and how good is a timely word!*" (Prov. 15:23). "*A word fitly (aptly) spoken is like apples of gold in settings of silver*" (Prov. 25:11).

Now that you have your top 8 goals establish, you are ready to talk to others. The KEY SECRET: Don't ask counselors what your goals should be. Don't ask them for their "opinion." Ask them to encourage and help you achieve what you already KNOW should happen. Make sure that those people you select are working toward YOUR predefined goals.

- Find people to speak into your life. Listen to them! Allow your mind to expand.

- Hire your weaknesses.

- Plan on how to build a team to reach your dream!

- In relationship to finances and investments, be accountable to someone (Mk. 9:35).

- Create connectivity to people.

- Ask for feedback.

- Drive collaborative efforts (Hab. 2:2).

- Don't try to be the Lone Ranger. Nobody is an island.

- Maintain teachabilty and be willing learn for your lifetime.

"Without counsel, plans go awry, but in the multitude of counselors, they are established" (Prov. 15:22).

It's far more essential to actually relate to people than try to impress people. *Believe it! Every single day be convinced that you have what it takes. Take the risk to believe and become extremely successful!*

Identify and List the Additional Resources You Need. What books should you read?

There are multiple resources available on all these subjects of building finances. If there is an area you are pursuing, get the information, education, certificates, and knowledge you need to accomplish your objective.

Who do you need to meet next?

Biblical mind-set on Accountability

Everyone needs someone to trust and to share their life with. Encouragement, counsel, and accountability are all imperative. Relational accountability is essential. Think in terms of 360 degree accountability - and you are like a brick. You have those above you, beside you, and below you. These will all help you take dominion and find true prosperity.

"And let us take thought of how to spur one another on to love and good works" (Heb. 10:24).

Commitment to others is the crucial element. As we demonstrate loyalty and dedication to the counsel from others, trust builds.

CONFESSION: *I am a favor magnet - people love to help me. I have incredible breakthroughs, divine encounters, profitable business ideas, restoration of energies, and the holy fire of Glory invades my life!*

Work on DOING your goal list! Say, "My life is worth living well."

"Put off for one day, and ten days will pass. ~ Korean Proverb

Day 37 - Focus on Reaping Prosperity!

"To accomplish great things, we must not only ACT, but also DREAM; not only PLAN, but also BELIEVE." – Anatole France

The wealthy tend to believe in themselves and what they do. Rich people are anxious to promote themselves and what they do. Poor people are cautious about self- promotion and restrained about aggressively marketing their products.

Every act of consumption creates a need for product. Wealthy people tend to sell what the market demands - and they sell to the masses rather than the few.

The rich regard exchanging money as an energy flow and they get into the flow that is happening. Sometimes, their way of doing things may seem shocking or sudden – and this uncanny momentum is one reason why they get spectacular results.

The Scripture tells us that "Faith is the substance of things not seen..." The rich person has perceptions that manifest reality or substance to their thoughts. Something happens! People want what they have.

Remember this

Affluence is a state of BEING. Having abundance begins with... abundance. You must desire it, accept it, want it, be comfortable with it. The wealthy see money as an energy kingdom that can be used for good. It can also cause you to reach your potential and find more enjoyment in life.

Believe that you are the best! Love what you do! Create conditions that resonate with this idea. Perpetuate the "feelings" of abundance. Your mental shift into subconscious awareness of abundance calls forth more abundance.

Cast your bread upon the water and it does return. The Law of Giving says that as you sincerely do good things that are in the will of God, you will receive the same of the Lord (Eph. 6:6-8). Give and it is given to you (Lk. 6:38).

Belief and faith brings life to whatever you focus upon. What you focus upon becomes magnified. You possess the ability that God gave you - to create your life. You tend and guard your garden with creative ability. When you feel like you *already* have something, it creates an agreement with gaining what you want.

"For I say unto you, That unto every one which has shall be given; and from him that has not, even that he has shall be taken away from him" (Luke 19:26).

Sowing & Reaping

The Law of Sowing and Reaping has been with us from the beginning - the whole plan of redemption is linked into this Truth. God redeemed the world back as He gave His Son. Jesus was His seed that died and rose again... so that there will be many sons returning to HIm.

"When I am trusting and being myself as fully as possible, everything in my life reflects this by falling into place easily, often miraculously." S. Gawain

Maximum prosperity is about BEING-ness.

If you believe you are poor, no matter how much money you ever make, you will always continue to be poor - because you're poor in heart. Because you have a mentality. Your awareness defines your Being. Remember.... it is all about being-ness. BEING is about having.

I imagine and say – therefore I am. I am therefore I have.

Deuteronomy 27:12-28 tells how half of the Israelite tribes stood on Mount Gerizim shouting the blessings of obedience to God's covenant -- while the other half stood on Mt. Ebal pronouncing the curses of disobedience. Do you see how what was in their mouth created their attitude of either blessing or cursing? How does this story help you find the intention of God for your life?

Are you aware that sometimes you are not fully productive? Observe your actions and responses. Learn to be the best!

What is unproductive in your life?

Be self aware - use self observation. Don't get caught up in problems. Deal with issues right away. Don't waste time and energy. Get it done. Find the solution and decide how to enhance your success rate. Take that Quantum Leap! You've got what it takes!

Don't just be a hearer but a DOER also (Jms. 1:22).

Do It!   CONFESSION: *God is making me an instrument of wealth.*

Write your NEW detailed plan to save money for your future.

You need to set up an emergency fund, write a livable budget, pay off smallest debts first, and then carefully invest in understandable investments such as mutual funds. Learning these principles takes time and application. But, it is necessity!

Try using the calculator at www.cnnmoney.com to find out how much you need to meet your goals, start a business, or to retire. Make your plan tangible.

"Financial intelligence is not so much how much money you make, but how much money you keep." Rich Dad

Where can you learn about making maximized investments?

Learning the skill sets to grow and keep money is a huge requirement! Money must become your servant.

CAUTIONS: Never make an emotional decision on investments - no quick schemes. No "now or never" pressure deals. Just because the person offering uses religious phrases or King

James grammar, doesn't mean it's a good deal! Christian-ese does not necessarily make an offer viable.

"If it sounds too good to be true, it probably is!"

- Use discernment. Never move out of a sense of urgency from another person. Use self-control.

- Find out what you need to know before investing. Use due diligence. Do a background check on the company and salesperson. Investigate.

- Get a return policy in case you change your mind.

- Don't exceed or over extend. Get wise counsel.

- NEVER put all your eggs in one investment.

- Prophetic words must be investigated, evaluated, and studied.

- Get all promises in writing. Use a legal contract written by a real lawyer. Make sure the contract is only about a specific investment. Make sure your money is held in escrow account. Make sure the contract has a return date for the investment promised.

- Write the check to a corporation not a person.[1]

"For I know the thoughts and plans that I have for you, says the Lord, thoughts and plans for welfare and peace and not for evil, to give you hope in your final outcome" (Jer. 29:11 AMP).

Spending or Saving

Benjamin Franklin talked a lot about careful spending - not to diminish your life-style, but being sure to save for the future. It is called "deferred consumption" where you invest for the future. Save some now for later.

Begin to appreciate what you have right now. Be diligent to live as fully and completely as possible on what you already have.

Having things is not wrong - just not your main reason for prosperity. Your primary purpose for prosperity is to establish the Kingdom of God in this earth!

1.*This list adapted from "Proceed with Caution" by Ap. John P. Kelly*

BEING prosperous means that you focus on DOING rather than OWNING more things. Prosperity allows you to enjoy life. Gaining more and more things is not usually the answer. Go places. Create memories. Have fun. Enjoy life. Focus on BEING & DOING rather than owning.

Be Happy in BEING, not just having! BE! You are created to prosper.

If you don't enjoy what you have now, how can you be happy later? The more you decide to be happy, the more you will have stuff to be happy about.

List what new things you really need to own? Not just more "things!"

What are the things you want to DO and where are the places you want to go?

What is your NEXT career going to be? Think beyond tomorrow.

What are you grateful for?

Every day say, "My life is worth living well."

Are you DOING your list?

"The trick is to get fired up and wired up, and become sacrificial to win, living like no one else, so that later you can live like no one else." Dave Ramsey

Day 38 - Focus on Prosperous Giving

"Faith is ready to use money to love people, it never uses people to get money." Kenneth Copeland

Inexhaustible Supply

While the news speaks of depression, exhausted supply, and lack, God's invisible supply is totally inexhaustible. The mountains and creeks are filled with undiscovered gold. There are unlimited riches in every unimaginable form coming toward you as fast as you can apprehend them.

There is ample abundance for everyone. That means you never strive, or contend, or compete with anyone else. You must never yield to wanting to have power or position over somebody else.

You create and apprehend what is intended to be yours. Nobody can take what is yours away from you. But you can give to them.

People learn to be wealthy by creating from within themselves, not by competition. Competition wants to keep others poor while wealth wants to create ways to inspire and empower others. Giving to others cooperates with God's vision for their lives.

God is NOT "about to" or "fixing'" to bring you money - He has already provided all that you need.

The Lord set the standard. You only advance as you increase in your present assignment. The more you give and are generous, the more you get. It is about sowing and reaping.

"The Lord has pleasure in the prosperity of his servant"
(Ps. 35:27).

Biblical Prosperity propels us to give! Luke 14:33 tells us that everything belongs to the Lord. God doesn't just claim the tithe. Everything we have should be directed by Him. Be aware of the fact that every day (right now) you create your own reality.

Now that you have learned to love yourself, you can focus on loving and giving to others. You have the means to show them the Gospel of love. This is just a brief overview on how giving relates to your prosperity.

You don't need a "leading" to give, sow, and pay tithes and offerings. Just do it! And, when the Spirit "leads" you beyond that – is when great things begin to happen.

"Now He who supplies seed to the sower and bread for food will also supply and increase your store of seed and will enlarge the harvest of your righteousness. YOU WILL BE MADE RICH IN EVERY WAY SO THAT YOU CAN BE GENEROUS ON EVERY OCCASION, and through us your generosity will result in thanksgiving to God" (2 Cor. 9:11-12, NIV).

You Give To Leaders

I know this is a touchy subject for some believers. There's been much abuse in the area of giving to leaders - and many people are reluctant to trust again. The issue is, you need to find those you can trust and give to them!

Many in ministry have no income other than from the work that they do to minister to you. You need to interact with those leaders who can help you achieve your desired objective.

Sometimes believers attempt to evaluate their leaders and decide that they already have "enough" money. Thinking that, they decide to give to someone else who appears to need money more. The deal is, you WANT to sow into someone who is prosperous so that they can help teach you to become more prosperous.

Abundant mind-sets KNOW that there is always plenty of money and the more you give the more can flow to you. It's like a river. The world is flowing in money like Niagara falls. If you give away teaspoon you're out of the flow. If you hold onto your stuff, the dam backs up and the river stagnates.

Nothing speaks of prosperity more than giving. Giving says that you know that God is the Source of all things. Giving is the expression in the flow of abundance – it tells everyone that your trust is not in yourself but in the Creator of all things.

"A greedy man stirs up dissension, but he who trusts in the Lord will PROSPER! (Prov. 28:25).

Release brings multiplication! Giving is a blessing of Faith in action. Giving is a Divine principle that releases God's energy!

I took the message of prosperity to the poorest villages in the Philippines after Pinatubo erupted. The best way to help the poor is to teach them to give money! Yes... the poor need to give. Poverty isn't stronger than abundance. Poor people didn't just need charity (although we took a plane load of provisions with us); they needed truth and inspiration. This is the Good News Gospel that everyone needs; abundance and increase will help change the world.

Giving isn't getting less for yourself. Remember this, sacrificial giving is not the entire Gospel -- but it is essential. Everything does depend on it. Truth resonates truth! Demonstrating the love of giving to others aligns yourself to prosperity. Your heart will sing harmoniously with unity and synchronicity.

- God owns everything. He gives us everything we have.
- God expects us to wisely steward all that He gives to us.
- He holds us accountable for how we use our money.
- Your spending decisions matter.
- Your giving duplicates God's character.
- Your giving should increase as time goes by.
- Your calling is to be a WEALTH DISTRIBUTOR. You must commit to that plan.

Unfortunately, many people get so wrapped up in pursuing their goals that they don't make plans to give something back.

Remember to be a faithful blessing to those who have sowed into your life to get you to where you are. Remember your spiritual mentors - they deserve a part of your harvest. You should give to the PERSON personally - and not just to their ministry. Remember those who speak into your life, mentor, and encourage you.

If you determine to allow the Holy Spirit to "lead" you in regard to your giving, keep in mind that the tithe is the least that He would say!

You don't give just to receive a reward! Come on! You give because you believe in the God of abundance. That's why Malachi says the windows of heaven open - because of unselfish motivation.

2 Corinthians 9:6-11 teaches us that "He that ministers seed to the sower both minister bread (the sustenance of the Word) for your food, and multiply your seed sown, and increase the fruits of your righteousness." That's a huge truth - if someone can impart the truth of the word to you AND multiply the seed that you sow... then that's the person to whom you should give.

- Keep in mind that there is both *seed* to sow and *bread* for food. BOTH are important. You need seed to sow and grow more and you need bread for your own sustenance.

- If you plant an entire peach, you will not get more harvest than planting just the seed. There is some that is intended for you to eat!

- Planting that seed gives you lots more plants with both food and seed. One planted acorn becomes a forest.

Remember the widow woman who gave her mite in the offering - we know from that story that it isn't about the amount but about giving sacrificially of your life. Sometimes giving is money, sometimes it is time or service. Giving is covenantal language.

"Again I tell you, if two of you on earth agree (harmonize together, make a symphony together) about whatever (anything and everything they may say, it will come to pass and be done for them by My Father in heaven" (Mat. 18:19).

"Can a man be profitable to God? Surely he that is wise is profitable to himself" Job 22:2

"A generous man will prosper..." (Prov. 11:25).

"Honor the LORD with thy substance, and with the first fruits of all your increase: So shall thy barns be filled with plenty, and thy presses shall burst out with new wine" (Prov. 3:9-10).

"...If you'll just help enough people get what they want, you'll never have to worry about what you want." Zig Ziglar

You should GIVE to your CHURCH

God wants to prosper ministries and ministers through your giving. That's the way it goes. Giving is how God finances the church and ministries. Ministries and churches get paid through your giving. Be sure you invest in places that are Kingdom minded and reaching out.

You should GIVE in WORSHIP

In the Old Testament, Israel knew that it was essential to bring offerings as worship to the Lord. Fortunately, we don't need to bring sheep, doves, or grain to church, but we need to remember that giving is a wonderful way to worship God.

Giving is all about attitude and motive. We don't give to get - we give because it is RIGHT to give. Giving lays up treasure in heaven (Matt. 6:19).

You should GIVE to IMPACT the KINGDOM.

Find opportunities for outlandish giving!

Church must move beyond the four walls and out into our cities and nations. Decisive apostolic strategies can refurbish slums and influence nations. We become the answer to the financial problems of the world. We have answers for recession, inflation, and lack.

When you give of your prosperity, you gain the ability to INFLUENCE.

You Should GIVE to HELP the POOR.

> "*He who gives to the poor will lack nothing, but he who closes his eyes to them receives many curses*" (Prov. 28:27).

> "*Tell them to use their money to do good. They should be rich in good works and generous to those in need, always being ready to share with others*" (1 Tim. 6:18).

> "*He who trusts in himself is a fool, but he who walks in wisdom is kept safe. He who GIVES to the poor will lack nothing, but he who closes his eyes to them receives many curses*" (Prov. 28:26-27).

You should GIVE in HARD TIMES:

> Genesis 26 tells us about a famine in the land when Isaac started to ask for help from Abimelech (the Philistine king of Gerar). The Lord appeared saying, "*Don't go down to Egypt.*" We find out that Isaac obeyed and stayed where he was.

> "*Then Isaac sowed in THAT land (where he was) and reaped in that SAME YEAR a hundredfold; and the Lord blessed him.*" (Gen. 26:18-23).

> Isaac obeyed and he became "very prosperous." Like Isaac, you have been given a land of assignment. YOU ARE NOT TO LEAVE your place of assignment.

- Build an altar there. Be settled and worship there.

- Remember to BOTH sow and give offerings. Don't stop just because of difficulty! Give to sow – not hoard.

- Be a cheerful giver!

- Find good soil to plant a seed - then from that one seed grow a forest.

- Pitch your tent. Be established in the place of your assignment and take dominion over your territory.

- Follow God's plan not yours.

- No matter what things look like, don't quit!

- Dig the well again. There is water in that place. Keep digging deep wells.

"A generous person will prosper. He who refreshes others will himself be refreshed" (Prov. 11:25).

El Shaddai, means the God Who is "More than enough!" His is total abundance. We are the image of a giving God - we give toward effectively expanding the Kingdom. Paul affirms this:

> God... *"Richly provides us with EVERYTHING FOR OUR ENJOYMENT. Command them to do good, to be rich in good deeds, and to BE GENEROUS AND WILLING TO SHARE. In this way they will lay up treasure for themselves as a firm foundation for the coming age, so that they may TAKE HOLD OF THE LIFE THAT IS TRULY LIFE"* (1 Tim 6:17-19).

"The Lord takes pleasure in the prosperity of His servants" (Ps. 35:27).

In your notebook, write out a definite plan to give financially to your spiritual leader, your church, and poor (and missions). What is God's will for you regarding sowing into Prosperity?

CONFESSION: *Those I bless are blessed. I see myself successful. Nations are blessed by me. God's power in me is attractive. That means I can help. Jesus is preeminent in my life. Therefore, all grace is abounding toward me.*

I can have a supply in every area of my life to give into every good work of God. I am a giver. I am a sower. Therefore, I am a reaper. Harvest day has arrived. Jesus became poor on the cross so I could be rich. Prosperity is part of the atonement and my spiritual right.

I resist lack and poverty in Jesus name. I will not live below my covenant rights I AM PROSPEROUS. Today will be a good day... This day, I am more than a conqueror. Today will be filled with blessings from God. All spiritual and natural blessings for this day have been arranged for me before the foundation of the earth. I can't lose.

What are you grateful for?   Work on DOING your list!

Day 39 - Focus on Established Prosperity

For much of this book, we've been climbing out of an old mind-set, one steeped in religious doubt and years of dulling and numbing discouragement about God's plan for prosperity. Now that merely surviving and getting by are no longer enough, we search for better ways to move forward.

Sometimes, progress can be difficult because of our thoughts about success and about what we deserve began in earliest childhood. It is a huge step to begin to continuously reprogram our mind to establish more correct concepts about God's intention of prosperity.

Life in the Spirit is all about LIFE (not death). It's all about being energized. Don't look back at the past one more time! Look ahead with anticipation.

My friend, IF you underestimate your potential, you will stay deprived, anesthetized, and underprivileged. But when you are convinced of who you are IN CHRIST, then what you have perceived as obstacles, now become the sturdy but flexible pole that you can use to vault over every hurdle.

Riches &
honor come
with wisdom
Prov. 3:16, 8:18

Remember
this

You are a spiritual person who is moving toward greater spiritual realization. Revelation awaits your open understanding! The Holy Spirit will guide you and change you.

Become razor-sharp with expectation. Renew that old man and dust off past limitations. Leap forward to your potential.

Dominion success is who you are - your DNA is programmed to achieve.

There are no limits for your life except for those you accept. Believe it! Every single day be convinced that you have what it takes. Take the risk to believe and become extremely successful!

Remember.... What will stop your progress?

- An unrenewed mindset
- Mediocrity
- Poverty mentality
- Fear and rejection
- Unforgiveness
- Uncertainty
- Negative thinking and negative words
- Doubt and unbelief
- Poor self-image and self-esteem
- Unfocused plans
- Lack of enthusiasm

The biggest opposition in your life is your own mind. Your mind is the thermostat that regulates success. If there is a limit on your life, it is internally set.

God wants you to prosper - He hasn't changed His mind. Focus on fulfilling your life. The best thing you can do for yourself is to live a life of hope, energy, positive thinking, desire, passion, and happiness!

Success and prosperity do not come magically, but only through consistent application of fundamental principles. Practice these all day every day. Do the right thing. Think positively. Stick to your goals.

Elijah wasn't happy about going to Zarepath to have a widow sustain him (1 Kn. 17). Zarepath means a refinery. But, it was there at the place of refining, that Elijah learned to trust God to work through other people and to even feed him by ravens. He experienced a supernatural exchange and sustenance through unexpected means.

Every day say, "My life is worth living well."

In order to achieve anything you must:

- Believe.
- Have purposeful (intentional) actions.
- Know that EVERYTHING MATTERS! Ask, "What's next?"
- Hold positive, yet flexible expectations.
- Present yourself as you see yourself finished and fully loved!
- Follow up. Follow up on your goals. Follow up. SET follow up plans on your calendar.
- Always look for better ways to do things. Is there something missing?
- Prioritize. Get help. Outsource. Delegate.
- Set aside time every day to pray and to just think.
- Remember who you are in Christ. Treasure your life. Value your time.
- Find joy, happiness, and contentment.
- Be prepared. Be positive. Be informed. Be goal driven.
- Admit when you make mistakes.
- Love what you do.
- Ignore those who oppose you.
- Find mentors. Learn from others.
- Don't blame anyone else - take responsibility.
- Lead or follow or get out of the way!
- Be grateful. Give God the credit.

CONFESSION: *I determine to walk in forgiveness and wholeness.*

Day 40 - Focus to the Prosperous Finish Line

You may be disappointed if you fail, but you are doomed if you don't try. - Beverly Sills

From what you've learned here so far begin to think about your long life-term vision and goals for the rest of your life. Now that you have done this for your financial goals, you should be able to now do it for the rest of the important areas in your life. You will also need to take this same approach to develop your physical goals, educational goals, career goals, family goals, savings goals, community goals, church goals, and recreational goals.[1] Everything you do in life should enhance your Vision!

Break it all down into bite sized pieces and write detailed goals for every week, every month, and every year. Then project out to five years and ten years.

What are the things you STILL can't change?

Success is a journey not a destination. - Anonymous

There are no secrets to success. It is the result of preparation, hard work, and learning from failure. - Colin Powell

• **Focus on how to finish each project that leads to vision.**

1.See my the Workbook, "On Getting There." for Understanding Wisdom.

- Help others be successful.

- Sincerely listen to others and be non-judgmental.

Biblical mind-set about Finishing

"And the Lord said to the faithful STEWARD... "Blessed (happy and to be envied) is that servant whom his master finds so doing when he arrives. Truly I tell you, he will set him in charge over all his possessions" (Lk. 12:42-44).

"For everything there is a season, and a time for every matter under heaven" (Ecc. 3:1, RSV).

Notice how all the facets of your life come together. Life comes together when you are consistent and don't quit. You must live a purpose driven life that focuses on meeting predetermined goals and fulfilling expectations.

Here, you find an absence of contradictions. There should be an agreement and synergy – a congruency that aligns your feelings, and an alignment of your thoughts, emotions, and actions.

1. Be proactive. Commit to your vision and goals. Live it. Rehearse it.

2. Examine and adjust your confession. Correct your faulty vocabulary and use of expressions. Speak intentionally with truth.

3. Continue to enlarge your belief and value system. Find Scriptures to back up your dream.

4. Build your life on the proper Biblical mindset.

5. Unleash your God-given intuition and imagination.

6. Trust your newly developed instincts. Become inspired to dream bigger.

7. DO IT NOW. Don't wait for conditions to seem right. Everything you do matters.

8. Learn to leverage your time.

Always remember that destiny isn't striving to accomplish self-centered goals. Grace demands no self-effort. No striving. The servant of the Lord must not strive!

Access your God given destiny. What you "do" is simply an outgrowth of becoming who you are meant to be. You apprehend your Godly vision and then begin to access your destiny through logical steps. You must continue to decide what to do and when and in what order! It's not about doing the URGENT things that always interrupt... it's about being compelled to DO the important things that relate to your objectives.

Learn to say "NO" to other things in order to obtain your dreams. Drive to the completion of the important.

"If they obey and serve him, they shall spend their days in prosperity, and their years in pleasures" (Job 36:11).

Summary

Money is a vehicle that helps to meet your needs and to supply the Kingdom. The Lord loves to bless you financially. He blesses you because you are His child. God opposes you when you TRUST in money as your source or objective of life.

Prosperity is the result of the Word of God operating in your life. The Scriptures clearly say that it is not God's will for any to perish, nor to live in sickness or poverty.

Move away from the past and don't look back. Don't be like Lot's wife! Don't keep talking about the problems in your life. Put all thoughts of poverty behind you. Ignore religious theories of doom. Keep away from books and movies about apocalyptic end time nightmares, and powerful demonic influences. The devil doesn't win, read the end of The Book!

Every law of the universe aligns when consistently purposeful action moves toward God's intention for your life!

The advancing believer maintains present action.

- Stop daydreaming and build on your God-given vision NOW.

- Behave as a citizen of God's expanding Kingdom.

- Guard your thoughts and words.

- Get a proper Biblical mind-set about prosperity.

- Don't wait for every thing to change before you change.

- Don't wait - ACT, DO IT NOW.

- Remember that increase always seeks greater expression.

- Every action should lead to your vision.

- Live in the present moment.

- Don't worry about yesterday (good or bad).

- Work for today with everything you can do. Do what matters for this day.

- Be excellent and work to full potential - don't rush or do sloppy work.

- Maintain FOCUS on your vision at all times.

- Don't try to do tomorrow's work today.

- It's not the number of things you do but the excellency and efficiency you do them.

- Do things immediately and fast, but not hastily.

- Make the changes you need NOW.

- Be grateful. Don't boast or take the credit!

- Don't allow discouragement, fear, or doubt.

- Believe you are on the right course - and proceed.

- Don't dwell on the possibility of failure.

- Don't talk about how hard it is or how tired you are.

- If you should ever fail, ask for a bigger dream.

- Encourage others to increase and succeed.

- Convey to others that you are confident, advancing, successful, and increasing.

- Don't permit anxiety, stress, or frustration. Be unwavering in Faith.

- Allow your peace to communicate success.

- Always give more value than people expect or pay for.

- Don't seek power over others.

- Steadily persevere and don't quit!

- Allow the POWER of vision and purpose to radiate from your thoughts, words, and countenance.

- Know that YOU can have abundance.

More Scriptures

"By humility and the fear of the Lord are RICHES, AND HONOR, AND LIFE" (Prov. 22:4).

"A faithful man shall abound with blessings" (Prov. 28:20).

"Keep therefore the words of this covenant, and do them, that ye may prosper in all that ye do" (Deut. 29:9).

"In the house of the righteous is much treasure, not much poverty!" (Prov. 15:6).

"The rich rule over the poor, and the borrower is servant to the lender" (Prov. 22:7).

"...Those that seek me early shall find me. Riches and honor are with me; yea, durable riches and righteousness.... That I may cause those that love me to inherit substance; and I will fill their treasures" (Prov. 8:17-18, 21).

"Let them shout for joy, and be glad, that favor my righteous cause: yes, let them say continually, Let the Lord be magnified, which has pleasure in the prosperity of his servant" (Ps. 35:27).

"See a man diligent in his business? he shall stand before kings; he shall not stand before mean men" (Prov. 22:29).

"The hand of the diligent makes rich" (Prov. 10:4)

"The thoughts of the diligent tend only to plenteousness" (Prov. 21:5).

"For with the same measure that ye mete withal it shall be measured to you again" (Lk. 6:38).

"Save now, I beseech you, O Lord: O Lord, I beseech you, send now prosperity" (Ps. 118:25).

"Honor the Lord with thy substance, and with the first fruits of all your increase: So shall thy barns be filled with plenty, and thy presses shall burst out with new wine" (Prov. 3:9-10).

Paul spoke of our greatest treasure, *"the riches of the glory of the inheritance IN THE SAINTS."*

"Blessed is the man Who walks not in the counsel of the ungodly, Nor stands in the path of sinners... He shall be like a tree Planted by the rivers of water, That brings forth its fruit in its season, Whose leaf also shall not wither; And whatever he does shall prosper" (Ps. 1:1-4).

Take your place - live in overflow!

How can you set a better example?

What are you grateful for?   Work on DOING your list!

Say, "My life is worth living well. My dreams are important."

CONFESSION:

I am part of the fellowship of the outspoken and unashamed!
My decision is made. I have stepped over the line.
My face is like a flint. My walk is pressing forward
to the high calling of Christ Jesus. My road is narrow.
My way may be rough, and my companions few.
My mission is clear.

I cannot be bought, sidetracked, detoured, lured away,
turned back, diluted, or delayed.
I won't look back, slow down, back away or be still.
My past is redeemed and my present makes sense.
My prosperous future is secure. I am finished with low living,
doubt talking, fear walking, small planning, colorless dreams,
uninteresting visions, mundane chatter, chintzy giving, and
dwarfed goals!

The Spirit of Death has no power over me.
I don't need man's approval, distorted success,
self exaltation, or popularity.
I don't need to be first, tops, recognized, praised or rewarded.
I won't give up, shut up, let up or slow up.
I am not offended.

I live by faith, love by patience, and exist by prayer.
I do not flinch in sacrifice, hesitate in adversity,
negotiate with the enemy, or wallow in the maze of mediocrity.
I keep on going cause I'm prayed up, paid up, stored up,
and filled up with the Holy Ghost.
I'm ransomed by His blood, and walk in the Spirit of Life.
I'll work until He comes and give it all I've got.
dks

> *"I will make you*
> *PROSPER*
> *more*
> *than before..."*
> *Ezk. 36:11*

Focus on Getting There #1

GOAL #1 *OBJECTIVE: What I am going to achieve!*

Write one clearly defined Goal that is measurable and uses action verbs.

I will_____

_____

_____

_____

_____

_____

WHYs & What I expect!

Prioritize the three main reasons WHY you want or need to accomplish this goal

1._____

2._____

3._____

Actions (tasks, strategies, STEPS, resources)

Write the five main activities you need to do to accomplish this goal. Add date to finish.

Steps Activity	Target Date	X

1.	
2.	
3.	
4.	
5.	

Build a mental and verbal picture of what you want. Write it down.
Say it and DO it!
Testify when it is completed.

Focus on Getting There #2

GOAL #1 *OBJECTIVE: What I am going to achieve!*
Write one clearly defined Goal that is measurable and uses action verbs.
I will_____

_____

_____

_____

_____

WHYs & What I expect!

Prioritize the three main reasons WHY you want or need to accomplish this goal
1._____

2._____

3._____

Actions (tasks, strategies, STEPS, resources)

Write the five main activities you need to do to accomplish this goal. Add date to finish.

Steps Activity	Target Date	X

1.		
2.		
3.		
4.		
5.		

Build a mental and verbal picture of what you want. Write it down.
Say it and DO it!
Testify when it is completed.

Focus on Getting There #3

GOAL #1 *OBJECTIVE: What I am going to achieve!*
Write one clearly defined Goal that is measurable and uses action verbs.
I will_____

_____

_____
_____
_____

WHYs & What I expect!

Prioritize the three main reasons WHY you want or need to accomplish this goal
1._____

2._____

3._____

Actions (tasks, strategies, STEPS, resources)

Write the five main activities you need to do to accomplish this goal. Add date to finish.

Steps <u>Activity</u>	<u>Target Date</u>	X

1.
2.
3.
4.
5.

Build a mental and verbal picture of what you want. Write it down.
Say it and DO it!
Testify when it is completed.

Focus on Getting There #5

GOAL #1 *OBJECTIVE: What I am going to achieve!*

Write one clearly defined Goal that is measurable and uses action verbs.

I will_____

_____

_____

_____

_____

_____

WHYs & What I expect!

Prioritize the three main reasons WHY you want or need to accomplish this goal

1._____

2._____

3._____

Actions (tasks, strategies, STEPS, resources)

Write the five main activities you need to do to accomplish this goal. Add date to finish.

Steps Activity	Target Date	X
1.		
2.		
3.		
4.		
5.		

Build a mental and verbal picture of what you want. Write it down.
Say it and DO it!
Testify when it is completed.

Focus on Getting There #6

GOAL #1 *OBJECTIVE: What I am going to achieve!*

Write one clearly defined Goal that is measurable and uses action verbs.

I will_____

_____

_____

_____

_____

WHYs & What I expect!

Prioritize the three main reasons WHY you want or need to accomplish this goal

1._____

2._____

3._____

Actions (tasks, strategies, STEPS, resources)

Write the five main activities you need to do to accomplish this goal. Add date to finish.

Steps <u>Activity</u>	<u>Target Date</u>	X
1.		
2.		
3.		
4.		
5.		

Build a mental and verbal picture of what you want. Write it down.
Say it and DO it!
Testify when it is completed.

Focus on Getting There #7

GOAL #1 *OBJECTIVE: What I am going to achieve!*
Write one clearly defined Goal that is measurable and uses action verbs.
I will_____

_____

_____

_____

_____

WHYs & What I expect!

Prioritize the three main reasons WHY you want or need to accomplish this goal
1._____

2._____

3._____

Actions (tasks, strategies, STEPS, resources)

Write the five main activities you need to do to accomplish this goal. Add date to finish.

Steps Activity	Target Date	X
1.		
2.		
3.		
4.		
5.		

Build a mental and verbal picture of what you want. Write it down.
Say it and DO it!
Testify when it is completed.

Focus on Getting There #8

GOAL #1 *OBJECTIVE: What I am going to achieve!*
Write one clearly defined Goal that is measurable and uses action verbs.
I will_____

_____

_____

_____

_____

_____

WHYs & What I expect!

Prioritize the three main reasons WHY you want or need to accomplish this goal
1._____

2._____

3._____

Actions (tasks, strategies, STEPS, resources)

Write the five main activities you need to do to accomplish this goal. Add date to finish.

Steps Activity	Target Date	X
1.		
2.		
3.		
4.		
5.		

Build a mental and verbal picture of what you want. Write it down.
Say it and DO it!
Testify when it is completed.

Endnotes: Why 40 days?

Lent consists of the 40 days preceding Easter.

Negative forty is the temperature at which the Fahrenheit and Celsius scales correspond.

The rain (during Noah's day) fell for 40 days and nights (Gen. 7:4).

Israel ate Manna for 40 years (Ex. 16:35).

Moses was on the mountain with God 40 days and nights (Ex. 24:18).

A second time Moses was with God 40 days and 40 nights (Ex. 34:28).

Israel wandered in the wilderness for 40 years (Num.14:33-34).

Moses led Israel from Egypt at age 80 (2 X 40)

Moses died at age 120 (3 X40; Deuteronomy 34:7).

The spies searched Canaan for 40 days (Numbers 13:25).

40 stripes was the maximum whipping penalty (Deut. 25:3).

God commanded that the land rest for 40 years (Jud. 3:11, 5:31, 8:28).

The Israelite judge Abdon had 40 sons (Jud. 12:14).

Because of evil, Israel was given over to an enemy for 40 years (Jud. 13:1).

Eli judged Israel for 40 years (1 Sam. 4:18).

Goliath taunted Israel for 40 days (1 Sam. 17:16).

Saul reigned for 40 years (Acts 13:21).

Saul's son, Ishbosheth was 40 when he started to rule (2 Sam. 2:10).

David ruled over Israel for 40 years (2 Samuel 5:4, 1 Kings 2:11).

The holy place of the temple was 40 cubits long (1 Kings 6:17).

Each of the 10 lavers in Solomon's temple contained 40 baths of liquid volume (1 Kin. 7:38).

The sockets of silver were groups of 40 (Exodus 26:19 & 21).

Solomon reigned 40 years (1 Kings 11:42).

Elijah ate one meal that gave him strength for 40 days (1 Kings 19:8).

Ezekiel bore the iniquity of Judah for 40 days (Ezekiel 4:6).

Joash reigned 40 years in Jerusalem (2 Kings 12:1).

Egypt was desolate for 40 years (Ezekiel 29:11-12).

Ezekiel's temple was 40 cubits long (Ezekiel 41:2).

The courts in Ezekiel's temple were 40 cubits long (Ezra 46:22).

Nineveh had 40 days to repent (Jonah 3:4).

Jesus was presented at the Temple 40 days after his birth (Lk. 2:22).

Jesus fasted 40 days and nights (Matt. 4:2).

Jesus was tempted 40 days (Luke 4:2, Mk. 1:13).

Jesus bore 40 stripes and by these we are healed (Is. 53:5).

Forty days from Jesus' resurrection till his ascension into heaven (Acts 1:3).

40 years is considered a generation (Numb. 32:13, Heb. 3:8-10).

According to the Talmud, it takes forty days for an embryo to be formed in its mother's womb.

Women are pregnant for 40 weeks. Forty, therefore, Is a symbol of birth and change.

40 indicates the duration of a generation or a long period. It also symbolizes the death with oneself and the spiritual rebirth.

40 is also the value of the letter *mem*, which represents water.

40 is the customary number of hours in a regular workweek in many Western countries.

According to the Bible, 40 is the number of the waiting, the preparation or the test.

According to Saint Augustine, forty expresses the perfection "because the Law was given in ten commandments, then it is through the whole world that the Law has been preached, and the whole world is composed of four parts, Orient and Occident, South and North; therefore, by multiplying ten by four, we obtain forty..."

Credit & Acknowledgement

ideas of this book may be from copious notes from tapes, seminars, and internet articles collected over many years – unfortunately, not knowing some sources. Also, this book contains many of the ideas and words of authors listed in bibliography and others.

Selected information from these sources may be paraphrased, summarized, or used with their verbatim apt phrases, sections, and ideas. I am grateful for their research. My apologies for any inadvertent lack of documentation. Some references may not be by Christians. Some of this book comes from my book, "On Getting There." Some of it is taken from excerpts from my articles on the internet. As a board member of ICWBF, many thoughts were gleaned from those meetings. Thanks to Cliff Hancock for inspiring the book name. Cover idea by JaLana Walsh.

Please get my e-book "*On Getting There*" for details about balancing the rest of your goals. This E-book accompanies the text, *"Finding Wisdom"* both on http://kluane.org

Several ideas are from:
Blair, Gary Ryan, *100 Day Challenge & weekly action plan*. Confidence, courage, thoughts. excellence.
Eberlye, Harold, "*Christianity Unshackled*" Greek thought
Howard, J. Grant, "*Balancing Life's Demands*" Multnomah Press, 97266
Militier, Lee, various internet articles
Spake, Kluane, "*From Enmity to Equality*" Greek thought
Tann, Enoch, Ezine articles
Wattles, Wallace, "*The Science of Getting Rich*" 1910 prosperity Guide, vision, thoughts, words, etc.
htttp://mercola.com, Dr. Mercola, articles, goals, internet quotes, Wallace Wattles,
http://www.bibleinsong.com/*Promises/Spiritual_blessings/*
http://www.globalchristians.org/
"*The Bible and its Interpretations and its Translations*" © 2000-2002 by Orchid Land Publications - Energy Scriptures
Teachings from ICWBF Lectures and notes, Apostle John Kelly.

Picutres - Google images
http://www.mywindpowersystem.com/wp-content/uploads/2009/09/alternative-energy-ocean-wave.jpg, energy, Google images
http://people.brandeis.edu/~ndr/Wissembourg/Rampart.JPG rampart
http://www.undiscoveredscotland.co.uk/queensferry/forthroadbridge/images/bridge-450.jpg Bridge Google images

Helpful sites:
http://fdic.gov (financial education)
http://financial-education-icfe.org)save more, use wisely)
http://foundationforcrediteducation.org (Step-by-step consumer guide)
http://bibletools.org/index.cfm/fuseaction/Topical.show/RTD/cgg/ID/605/Gods-Rest.htm (rest)
http://investopedia.com
http://federalreserveeducation.org (Banking, trade, mortgages, Credit Cards, etc.)
http://money.cnn.com/magazines/moneymag/momey101 (guide to gain financial control)

CONTACT Dr. Kluane Spake

877-SPAKE-99   spake@mindspring.com

Mail: P.O. Box 941933 Atlanta, GA 31141

http://kluane.org   http://jubileealliance.com

http://the-Q.org   www.kluane.org/store

Dr. Kluane Spake has spent a lifetime teaching and training leaders and believers on how to apply the word to their daily lives and how to maximize their potential relevance and effectiveness. She is internationally recognized as an apostle, minister, author, mentor, scholar, educator, and friend to the Body of Christ. She is a pastor to pastors, and mentor.

SPEAKER: As a International Speaker, Dr. Kluane is an internationally recognized as a prophetic apostle who is Breaking the Stained Glass Ceiling! She teaches revelation on Finished Work, the Third Day Church, Melchizedek, Equality, Unity, Leadership, Present Truth, and where the church is going, etc.

*   Dr. Kluane Spake now travels in ministry world-wide preaching/teaching at local church services, conferences, crusades, and pastor's meetings. She is a scholar, author, and educator.

*   Dr. Kluane is also president and founder of Jubilee Inc, SWORD Ministries, Inc, and Jubilee Alliance (an apostolic network http://jubileealliance.com).

*   Founder of The Quickening Church, Norcross, GA and previosly pastor of Jubilee, a successful church in Guam.

*   President and founder of Jubilee Alliance, an apostolic network http://jubileealliance.com

*   Founder of SWORD Ministries, Atlanta, GA - apostolic traveling ministry.

*   Doctor of Theology and Doctor of Naturopathy

*   Member of the International Coalition of Apostles (ICA). Appointed Ambassadorial Apostle of ICA (J. P. Kelly)

- Ecclesiastical Board Member for the International Christian Wealth Builders Foundation– Apostle John Kelly

- Doctoral Diplomat in Christian Counseling International Association of Christian Counseling Professionals (IACCP)

- Licensed Life Coach with IACCP

- Advisory Counsel for the International Connection of Ministries - Bishop Kirby Clements (2010-11)

- Primary faculty and Ambassador for Vision International University--Dr. Stan DeKoven

- Board member for All Nations Church, Norcross, GA– Apostle Frank Offosu Appiah

- Board member, adviser, mentor, and consultant for several other ministries.

- FRIEND of God and to the Body of Christ.

She is Founder of Jubilee Alliance Apostolic Network and also the founder and overseer of "The Quickening Church" Norcross, GA http;//the-Q.org

AUTHOR. Dr. Kluane has written many compelling books including: "Connecting" Spiritual Realities; "Apostolic Authority" about new church government; "Whole & Holy," "Understanding Wisdom," "Understanding Headship," "Why I Speak In Tongues" and "In Defense of Respect, Honor, & Titles," "From Enmity to Equality," and several interactive study and manuals that implement principles of living a relevant life.

LEADERSHIP MENTOR & CONSULTANT. Founder of Jubilee Alliance Apostolic Network http://jubileealliance.com, Dr. Kluane encourages, coaches, and serves ministry leaders, empowering them to raise their organizations to the next higher level.

Made in the USA
Las Vegas, NV
30 April 2022